Walking

with Sue Gearing

West

WESTERN
Daily Press

West Country Walks

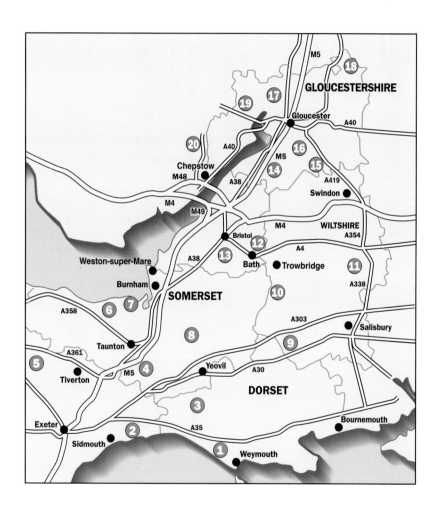

Inspect the Fleet

Chickerell – Langton Herring – Chickerell

About 6.75 miles. About 3.5 hours walking

Explorer Outdoor Leisure Map 15, Purbeck & South Dorset, map ref: 643 804

This is an exhilarating walk in Dorset coastal country once infamous for smuggling. It closely follows the Fleet, the unique lagoon and nature reserve at the back of the 29 mile long Chesil Beach in South Dorset. It's an easy, flat figure of eight ramble with  only gentle hills and a popular village inn en route and another in Chickerell. There is a wide variety of bird life, because the Fleet is a favourite wintering area, and there are many swans, maybe because of the nearby swannery at Abbotsbury. Look out also for partridges, corn bunting, whitethroats and many skylarks. Butterflies and wildflowers complete the interest and beauty of this ramble.

START at **Chickerell, about two miles west of Weymouth on the B3157.** Go down East Street and find somewhere to park there or turn left into West Street.

1 Chickerell – From East Street, turn into West Street and follow it up past the Lugger Inn to the main road. Turn left and at the roundabout, cross with care and take the lane towards Fleet. Soon pass distinctive gates with their arm and flag emblems at the entrance to Moonfleet Manor estate. Follow the lane straight down, glimpsing the water of the Fleet ahead. At the bend go left by East Fleet Farm on the coast path and here you may like to visit the Old Church at East Fleet. Only the chancel remains. The rest of the church was washed away in a fierce storm of 1824. Go along a line of cottages, over a stile and enter Fleet Nature Reserve. Follow the arrow to the coast path.

2 The Fleet – Reach the edge of the Fleet the largest tidal lagoon in the country. It is protected from the sea by Chesil Beach.

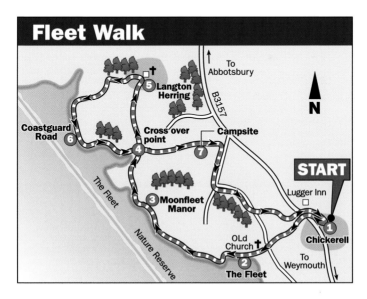

Fleet Walk

To Abbotsbury

N

5 Langton Herring

B3157

Coastguard Road 6

Cross over point

Campsite

4

7

START

The Fleet

Lugger Inn

3 Moonfleet Manor

Nature Reserve

OLd Church

Chickerell

To Weymouth

2

The Fleet

The area was used by Barnes Wallis during the 1940s to test the bouncing bomb. Because of the unique nature of the geology of this coast, it became the first designated World Natural Heritage Site in the country. Over 185 million years of the earth's history is represented in just 95 miles of coastline.

Go right over a stile to follow the water along the South West Coast Path.

❸ Moonfleet Manor – After about a mile and a half you come to Moonfleet Manor, now a luxury hotel and pass in front of it.

This area was the setting for 'Moonfleet', J. Falkner's famous children's novel about Dorset smugglers and contraband hidden in graves.

Don't miss the interesting information board about the Fleet Lagoon Nature Reserve.

Continue on in the Abbotsbury direction, and there is the option of going left down on to the shore of Gore Cove. Our route now leaves the water's edge and cuts inland across the back of the Henbury headland. Follow a wall on your right until you reach a footpath sign. This is the cross over point of our figure-of-eight walk. We now go in the Langton Herring direction and rejoin the edge of the Fleet later on.

4 Cross over point – Take the stony track which climbs steadily up to Langton Herring village. In the distance is the Memorial to Thomas Hardy on Black Down. Go through a metal gate and follow the lane to the village.

5 Langton Herring – The centre of Langton Herring is remarkably unspoilt and most of the buildings are constructed of local yellow stone. Many date from the 19th Century, but a few 18th Century thatched cottages still survive.

Turn right and come to another junction with the Elm Tree Inn, a firm favourite with walkers, on the opposite corner.

Turn left past St Peter's Church, a pretty church with a very small tower. Follow the lane down and round left and at a T-junction turn left on the bridleway. Follow the stony track and enjoy pleasant views over the valley. Go round a bend, ignoring the footpath on the bend. Shortly, take the next footpath on the right marked to Rodden Hive. Go diagonally left down the field with a truly panoramic view over Chesil Beach, along the coast and across the folding Dorset countryside. If the path is unclear make sure you aim for two low square buildings on Chesil Beach. Cross a stile down in the corner onto a steep narrow path. After crossing another stile, go right down the hedge line. At the bottom, turn left in the field with the Fleet on your right. Climb gently and continue along the Fleet to a kissing gate onto, Coastguard Road.

6 Coastguard Road – Cross and continue ahead along the Fleet. Eventually cross a footbridge and come back to the cross-over point.

Go right on the track for a few yards and then go left over a stile on the path up to Bagwell Farm campsite.

7 **Campsite** – Continue climbing up fields until you come into the campsite. Go straight ahead on the tarmac path. Pass the toilet block and follow the arrow straight on past caravans. At a T-junction of paths in the campsite go left towards the shop and then go right still following a campsite drive. At the bend head across to a stile onto a wide track. Turn right uphill. Join a concrete drive and continue on. Then you reach a T-junction with a tarmac lane. Turn left and follow it to a junction with a larger lane. Turn left downhill. Take the second footpath on the left through a gate just before a Give Way to Oncoming Vehicles sign. You may wish to make a few minutes detour down the lane to the small church of Chickerell with Fleet (locked at 4pm in winter).

To continue, follow the footpath down the field and over a stile in the corner. Go ahead and cross a stile/footbridge/stile and head diagonally steeply up across the field to the top. Cross the stile in the corner, enjoying a last view over the Fleet. Follow the hedge and cross a stile on the left. The path takes you along to the road where you were earlier. Turn left and retrace your steps back to Chickerell.

The Elm Tree Inn
Langton Herring.
Call: 01305 871257

The Lugger Inn
Chickerell.
Call: 01305 766611

Devon coastal walk

Salcombe Hill – Salcombe Mouth – Weston Mouth – Salcombe Regis
– Salcombe Hill

4.75 miles 3 hours walking

OS Explorer 115 Exmouth & Sidmouth, ref: 139 880

Wild flower meadows fringing red marl cliffs, beach, sea, big skies, coastal views and donkeys galore– these are the temptations on this quite strenuous coastal circle. Although short, some of the hills are a real challenge, but the changing and dramatic scenery makes it worthwhile. Much of the walking is across National Trust coastal land, and thankfully there are lots of benches for rests en route. Lunch or refreshments can be taken at the excellent Hay Loft restaurant of the fascinating Donkey Sanctuary about two-thirds of the way round or later at Salcombe Regis teas are served by the church on Sunday afternoons (2.45–6pm). Take your bathing costumes in case you want a swim at Salcombe or Weston Mouth beaches (stony).

1 **Salcombe Hill car park** – Take the signed 'Salcombe Hill cliff and link to coast path'. After a few yards reach a tarmac drive. Turn left and come to the entrance gate to a house where you take the path at the side, National Trust Salcombe Hill. Follow this dry stony path which gives tremendous views west along the coast over Sidmouth, especially if you take a detour towards the edge. Return to the main path signed to Salcombe Mouth. Go through a gate onto South Combe Farm land with a carved stone proclaiming,

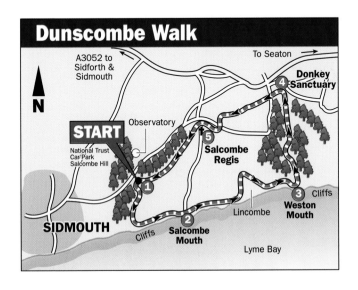

Dunscombe Walk

A3052 to Sidforth & Sidmouth

To Seaton

N

Donkey Sanctuary **4**

Observatory

START

National Trust Car Park Salcombe Hill

5

Salcombe Regis

3 Cliffs

1

Lincombe

Weston Mouth

SIDMOUTH

Cliffs

2

Salcombe Mouth

Lyme Bay

"No sounds of wordly toil ascending there, mar the full burst of prayer". Continue along the cliff edge and then ascend very steeply down steps to Salcombe Mouth.

2 **Salcombe Mouth** – At the signpost down in the combe, our route continues left towards Weston Mouth, but beforehand you can drop down to the beach at Salcombe Mouth if you wish.

Follow the edge of the combe for a short distance and turn right over a footbridge. Climb steeply up the field and then even more steeply to the top of Dunscombe Cliff. Take your time and enjoy the views as you get higher. Go along the top following the cliff edge and after about a third of a mile we have to turn inland to get round the combe. So follow the arrow inland and go across the head of the combe. At a signpost (broken when I came here) head out again to the cliff edge still heading for Weston Mouth.

Follow the grassy path through wonderful areas of wildflowers and then through woodland. Continue on the path to Weston Mouth dropping downhill again.

3 **Weston Mouth** – At the foot, you can go through the kissing gate and steeply down onto the beach.

To continue our circle turn left inland heading for Dunscombe following the stream on your right. Half way up the hill, fork right towards Slade House Farm and the Donkey Sanctuary.

4 **Donkey Sanctuary** – Reach the Sanctuary, a fascinating place to look round with fields full of donkeys. It's an opportunity to see them close at hand and learn about the history and aims of this Sanctuary. It is open every day of the year from 9am to dusk and admission is free. Dogs are welcome but must be firmly controlled on a lead. There is a Hayloft restaurant serving lunches, snacks, coffees,

teas and you can have a glass of beer or wine if eating there.

Go out the back of the Sanctuary on the Salcombe Regis path. This goes up the concrete path past car park P out to a lane. Turn left and immediately right through an aluminium 7-bar gate. Go ahead to a kissing gate and follow the right edge of the field to the corner. Go into the next field and continue ahead keeping parallel with the hedge over on the left. Half way down, go left over a stile and then right following the hedge on the

right, in the same direction as before. Cross a stile and head across the field and over another stile. Go ahead along the hedge, as before and at the corner, stay in the field turning left along the far hedge-line, following footpath arrow. Come out to a lane. Turn right and drop down to the pretty village of thatched cottages.

5 **Salcombe Regis** - The name 'Salcombe' comes from the salt works that used to exist at the mouth of the combe and 'Regis' commemorates the

Manor having been granted to the monastery in Exeter by King Athelstan (925-940).

At the junction in the village, turn left to the church. It is built of very fine Devon freestone (sandstone), built with the wealth derived from the wool industry which thrived in these parts after the Black Death. It is a peaceful and very friendly little centre with a satisfying square shape instead of the usual long chancel. The unusual engraved glass triptych by Simon Whistler behind the altar is particularly beautiful.

Continue on the lane past the church dropping gently down. Then fork up right on a track through a wooden barrier. This is the public footpath to Sidmouth (the sign is a yard further down the road on the left opposite a kissing gate which also leads to the path). This goes up steadily through woodland. At a crossing of tracks go straight over heading for Salcombe Hill car park. Reach a crossing track. Turn right, still in the woods, and shortly reach the car park.

Hayloft Restaurant
at the Donkey Sanctuary,
open Spring and Summer daily
10.30am – 4.30pm;
in Winter open
Tuesday-Sunday,
11.30am – 3.30pm.
Groups of walkers should
advise the restaurant when
they are coming so they can
stock up on soups or
whatever else hungry ramblers
might require!
Call: 01395 514996

Dorset hills & trails

Beaminster – Lewesdon Hill – Stoke Abbott – Beaminster

Just over 7 miles. About 4 hours walking

OS Explorer 116 Lyme Regis & Bridport, ref 481 014

It's hard to beat this walk from Beaminster if you want glorious Dorset countryside and spectacular views. Try and choose a clear day to enjoy the panorama as we climb two hills. In this West Dorset walk there are folds and hidden valleys, streams, shady beech woodlands, beautiful country cottages and a pretty village and welcoming pub en route. We also pass one of the country's new Community Woodlands. Our way is along the well-marked Ridgeway path and the not-so-well-marked Jubilee Trail for much of the time. Wear suitable shoes and clothes to walk through longish grass as it could be wet. Near the end we pass by stately Parnham House. There are steep sections, but they are well worth the climb.

Beaminster : WALK 3

START in Beaminster (pronounced Beminster), on the A3066 Crewkerne-Bridport road. Go to the main car park off the market square and through to the longer stay section − £1 per day.

Beaminster, situated at the head of the Brit valley, is a prosperous little market town which once thrived from wool cloth, sailcloth, sackcloth and shoe-thread, rope and twine. Then, over a period of a century and a half, it was devastated three times by fire, first in 1644 during the Royalist occupation, then in 1684 and again in 1781. As a result, few of the finest 17th Century houses survive, but it still has some fine Georgian buildings and picturesque 17th Century cottages, and the whole of the town's historic centre is a Conservation Area featuring over 200 listed buildings.

Beaminster Walk

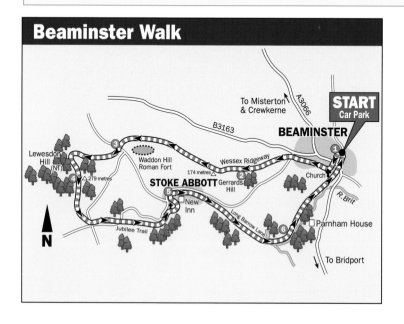

① Market Square - Walk back up to the market square and go down Church Street towards St Mary's Church. It's a beautiful 15th Century church which is manned by volunteers during the summer months to provide information and welcome visitors.

It is a light and airy church with an impressive monument to the Strode family of Parnham. I loved the large stitched tryptch at the back of the church based on Beaminster which was worked as a Millennium project.

Turn right on the lane just before the church, or if coming from the church, go out through the churchyard and turn left on the lane. Continue along here in the back of Beaminster along Shorts Road. Carry on along the footpath – the Wessex Ridgeway. Go through a metal gate by a bigger gate and ahead through a field – still on the edge of Beaminster. Cross a stile onto a lane. Turn left and almost immediately turn right on Halfacre Lane. Go left over a stile on the marked Ridgeway and walk diagonally up the field towards a farm at the top.

Cross a stile and ahead and round two sides of the barn keeping it on your left. Cross a double stile and drop downhill, over another stile and pass through a

plantation. Cross the stream on a foot-bridge and then go straight ahead up the field and take the path that forks up right, climbing steeply up Gerrards Hill, getting tremendous views. Pass an oak tree and continue up (don't fork right). Over a stile at the top, across a track and over another stile − still on the Ridgeway and still climbing.

2 Gerrards Hill - Head up to a copse of trees and pass it on your left − just before this there's a trig point over on the left at 174 metres. Now walk along the ridge where the air is exhilarating and the views are sweeping. Go through a gate

and continue on along the ridge with a fence on your right. Go through another gate getting near a farm and cross a stile and then cross the diverted, clearly marked Ridgeway which goes down steps, below the farm and then up steps on the other side. Go through a metal gate and then carry on along the hill. (For a good coastal view, make a small diversion taking the path alongside the cottage). Come back to the path along the hill with a fence on the right. Just carry on following the Ridgeway signs for about another half mile through fields, finally dropping down and going through Stoke Knapp Farm.

The humps and bumps up in the field on your left are part of the old Waddon Hill Roman Fort.

3 **Lane** – Reach a lane, cross onto the Wessex Ridgeway track opposite, starting to climb up to wooded Lewesdon Hill. This sunken, green and ferny lane is quite a contrast to the earlier walking. Reach a National Trust sign marking the start of the Hill and passing glorious beech woodland on your left which looks as though it would be full of bluebells in season. If the path is muddy you could walk parallel, in the woods themselves which are drier.

Reach a crossing footpath and another National Trust sign. Here leave the Ridgeway and go uphill on the path though the woods, steeply climbing up to the top of the hill (279 metres).

4 **Top of hill** – Go ahead along the top for a short distance only – so enjoy the views while you are there – and then follow the path straight ahead downhill. It is quite steep at first but then becomes more gentle. Near the bottom reach a crossing track. Go down right and after a few yards reach a junction with a concrete track. Go left and shortly cross a stile on the right into a field. Go across heading for the bottom left corner. Go through into the next field and straight ahead, aiming for a gate between the left far corner and a house. Having come onto a lane, turn left and it is a short step to a crossroads with the main road.

Go straight over on the Stoke Abbott lane, which is the route of the Jubilee Trail.

This is a 90 mile footpath from Forde Abbey to Bokerlye Dyke, opened in 1995 by the Ramblers Association to celebrate their 60th anniversary. (Sadly, some of this section of the Trail was not well marked when I came here.)

After about a third of a mile, at a left hand bend, go straight ahead to the right of a house on the Wessex Ridgeway. The path is a little overgrown at the start. Go past the farm, cross a stile and across a track and ahead into a field. Follow the right hedge and at the hedge corner go downhill steeply, bearing slightly left and look for a footbridge in the trees with a stile each end. Go up into a garden/field and climb steeply up aiming to the left of the cottage. Cross a stile and cross a track and take the steps and stile opposite. Head across this field to a stile and continue on in the same direction in the next field picking up a grassy track which drops down and goes through a gate to a stony track. Turn left and come to a junction with a lane.

5 **Stoke Abbott** – Turn right and soon reach Stoke Abbott, one of West Dorset's prettiest villages.

One of the village's claims to fame is that in 1858 James Searle committed a murder here and was the last person to be publicly hanged in England!

It's worth a tiny detour to go right down a track to St Mary's Church. I particularly liked the Millennium Window of the nativity in the north wall. It has a beautiful 12th Century font and a very noisy clock on the tower!

To continue, turn left out of the church on the path and then turn left and come back onto the lane in the village, where you turn right. If you didn't visit the church, you just stay on the lane.

Soon there is the welcoming sight of the New Inn. There is a sign explaining that the village used to be called Abbott Stoke and relates to a former dairy farm of the manor of the Abbots.

Continue on along the lane through the village, ignoring the Jubilee Trail which turns off on the right. We meet up with the Trail later. The lane drops downhill under trees and is decorated with ferns and ivy. Ignore the road right to Horsehill Farm and a little later take the marked track which forks to the right. This is an old thoroughfare called Long Barrow Lane.

6 **Community Wood** – Pass Little Giant Wood. One of 200 new community woods across England and Wales, was planted in 1999 with the help of local people and is open if you wish to explore.

Continue on the track which has now become the Jubilee Trail again. Follow it round a left bend and go along a section

track and across another stile into a field. Follow the arrow ahead down the field for quite a distance gradually making your way towards the right hand edge and going by an avenue of oak trees. Cross a stile onto a track and turn left.

The Jubilee Trail soon leaves us and goes right but you could make a small detour on this to go down, across the River Brit and along to Parnham House, now a private house and no longer open to the public but you can get a good glimpse of this beautiful old stately home.

Return to the path you were on and continue on as before through fields. Come out onto Parnham House drive and follow it ahead and come into Beaminster. At a T-junction turn right up to the main market square and cross to go down to the car park.

which may be rather overgrown. Follow the next directions very carefully as the way was not signed. Come into a field and follow the left hedge for a short distance until a point where the hedge kinks. Here, turn right and head across and down the field, to leave it in the bottom left corner and come onto a path in woodland.

Cross a footbridge and pick up a Jubilee Sign again. Follow the path through woods by the stream. Ignore the next footbridge and soon the Trail takes you through a hunting gate into a field. Proceed a few yards left along the edge and then head straight across the field going uphill. When you get to the brow continue across heading just to the right end of a distinctive clump of trees on the far side. Find the Jubilee Trail sign again on a stile which you cross. Go over the

The New Inn
Stoke Abbott.
Call: 01308 868333

Take me back
to the Blackdowns

Corfe – Adcombe Hill – Pitminster – Corfe

4.75 miles (or 5 miles by the lane)

Explorer 128 Taunton and the Blackdown Hills, ref: 231 194

This is a short walk in the Blackdown Hills, very close to
Taunton and easily accessible. The fascinating skeletons
of leaf-bare woodlands contrasting with the folding hills
make this a good walk for winter, as well as all year.
There's quite a lot of woodland walking and the circle links
you via tracks, lanes and fields with two Somerset villages,
Corfe and Pitminster. When in Pitminster see if you can
spot the slight lean in the church spire – and that's before
you visit the pub! There is one fairly steep uphill
stretch of about 20 mins to get to the top of
Adcombe Hill – but the views are a fine reward.
There are two routes up the hill – one up an old track
through woodland, where it is in parts uneven under
foot, or the other up the lane which is longer but
very quiet. Wear good footwear as in winter the
combination of leaves on paths where the stones
are quite large and loose can be slippery, and there
is one section which will be wet after rain.

START in the village of **Corfe on the B3170. Leave the M5 at Junction 25, Taunton turn-off.** Turn towards Taunton, go over roundabout and shortly at the lights, turn left following the B3170. At the next lights, turn left on the Ilminster Road, which is still the B3170 and continue to follow signs to Corfe, going over the M5 and passing Taunton racecourse. Park at the entrance to the village (Taunton side) either on the right in Newton Lane by the village hall and children's play area, or on the left down Mill Lane. Park carefully to avoid inconvenience to hall or church users.

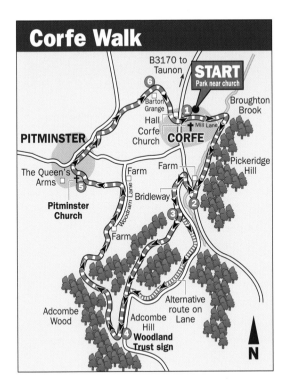

Corfe Walk

B3170 to
Taunon

START
Park near church

Broughton
Brook

Barton
Grange
Hall
Corfe
Church
CORFE
Mill Lane

PITMINSTER

Pickeridge
Hill

The Queen's
Arms

Farm
Farm

**Pitminster
Church**

Bridleway

Woodram Lane

Farm

Adcombe
Wood

Adcombe
Hill

Alternative
route on
Lane

**Woodland
Trust sign**

N

1 **Corfe church** – Note the splendid Celtic cross outside the church as a war memorial. St Nicholas Church is built in the Anglo Norman style.

Go down Mill Lane at the side of St Nicholas Church on the public footpath marked to Heale. Pass the Old Mill House and continue on down a track when the tarmac ends. Go through a large metal gate, and almost immediately at the bend, go straight ahead on the footpath. Follow the hedge on the left down the field with glimpses of Taunton on the left and head-ing towards a wooded hill – the slopes of Pickeridge Hill. Behind, there's a good view back to Corfe and the church. Go through a wooden kissing gate and go down the right side of the field with Broughton Brook bubbling away steeply down below.

Cross a footbridge over the stream and a stile into the field. Turn right, walking below the hill and with the brook on your right. Go ahead through several fields and eventually reach the end of the last field with a farm at the side. Go over the stile by the gate and turn right on the farm drive. Pass beautiful thatched Brook Farmhouse and reach the main road.

② Main road - Turn right. Take care as you go round the bend. After 1.5 minutes, cross the road and turn left up the first lane – Adcombe Lane. After about three minutes, having passed cottages, look for a bridleway sign in the hedge on the left directing you to the right up a house drive by a low chain link fencing with a beautiful Cedar of Lebanon tree in the garden.

③ Start of Bridleway - You can either take the bridleway, which is shorter or stay on Adcombe Lane. Pass closely to the right of the house, passing the front door, and go ahead through a gate onto a stony track in trees. Now follow this all

way steeply uphill, mainly in woodland. Go through a metal hunting gate by a large gate and continue on up the track to come out on to Adcombe Lane again near the top of the hill through another hunting gate. On a clear day there are wonderful views across the Vale of Taunton.

(If staying on the line follow it quite steeply uphill and then enjoy a flat section with great views just before you reach the metal gate at the top on the right by a slight bend.)

Continue along the lane out in the open now on the hill for about a fifth of a mile and begin gently to descend. Then reach woods on the right with a gate and a Woodland Trust sign.

④ Woodland Trust sign - Go through onto the broad track along the top of the wood with the trees plunging down the slope on your left. Stay on the top track – ignore the fork down left. Continue on this track for about three quarters of a mile, dropping down and leaving the woodland. By and large the path is good underfoot but after leaving the woods, the path

becomes stonier and narrow and after rain will be wet. Take care of your footing on this section . As you get near the stone farmhouse at the bottom the track improves. Bear round right by the farm and continue along the tarmac lane – Woodram Lane.

Pass a picturesque farmhouse on the left, Woodram. Not long after this, reach a farm on the right and opposite it go through the metal gate on the left. It is a footpath but unmarked at this stage. Follow the right hedge ahead heading in the direction of Pitminster church with its unusual lead-covered spire. Can you detect a slight tilt to the south? This apparently has been caused by distortion to some of the massive supporting timbers.

Cross a stile on the far side where it may be muddy after rain. Continue on as before in the next field along the right hedge. Cut off the far right corner and bear off to a stile and footbridge on the far side. Go straight across the next field and cross one footbridge followed immediately by another on the right. Turn right along the hedge and through a gate onto a lane. Cross over and go through a gate into Pitminster churchyard.

⑤ Pitminster Church – Dedicated to two saints, St Mary and St Andrew, it's a beautiful church well worth a visit. There was a building here in Saxon days but it was completely rebuilt by the Prior of Taunton and the Augustinian canons in the 13th Century. The tower dates from this time as do some parts of the nave. There are remarkable effigies in the church to the Colles family, owners of nearby Barton Grange which we pass later in the walk. The monuments are notable for the beauty of carving, costumes and the poetry of the inscriptions. There is a very informative guide book at the back of the church if you want to learn more. I particularly liked the modern window in the chancel showing Christ summoning Andrew on the shores of Lake Galilee which was designed and made by Jane Grey of Shropshire.

Leave the church by the main door and turn left leaving the churchyard through memorial iron gates. (If you don't go into the church, simply follow the churchyard wall on the left all the way round to

⑥ Barton Grange – This large mansion was built in 1538 by a wealthy entrepreneur, Humphrey Colles, who bought up farmlands belonging to Taunton Priory and which were sold off after the dissolution of the monasteries. It was built in a commanding position on a hill above the fish ponds which were part of a farm established by the Prior of Taunton and the Augustinian Canons.

the gates.) Go down to the village lane and bear right to arrive at the popular Queen's Arms on the corner in the village.

This has a full menu of home cooked food and is open every lunchtime for meals. The village name refers to the many pits where flint is extracted.

Turn right through part of the village and then fork left on the Poundisford lane, passing Littleham Cottages and then leaving the village. Cross a stream and continue on, ignoring a footpath on the right. After about six minutes from the pub, opposite Parkfields, go right up a footpath track . Follow this over a stream and head up to Barton Grange up on the top.

As you pass close by the Grange, look on the left for a wooden footpath sign marked to Corfe. Go into the field and follow the right hedge all the way along, round the end of the wall, round a corner and continue along. Go through an opening on the right, marked with a public footpath sign. Head diagonally right across the centre of the field heading towards the right hand end of the low village hall in Corfe where you may have parked.

The Queens Arms
Call: 01823 421529

Magic of the moor

Anstey Gate – Molland – Anstey Gate

Distance 5 miles. Walking time 2.5 hours

Ordnance Survey Explorer OL 9 (Exmoor National Park) Ref: 835298

Deer, ponies, buzzards and pheasant watch your progress on this Exmoor circle which goes from heather moorland down to a delightful small village on the southern slopes. Here, in Molland, famous for a rare lily, St Mary's church stands shoulder to shoulder with the delightful London Inn as symbols of English village life. The old, cosy pub itself is well worth the leg work. The food and atmosphere are memorable. This is a walk to surprise and delight, whether it is the widespread views and openness – particularly apparent in winter – the bewitching heather which covers the moor in summer and autumn, daffodlils which flourish around Molland, or the streams which bubble down through gulleys. It does have its ups and downs and there's a couple of steep but short stretches. So take your time and the effort is well rewarded. You will need good footwear as it may be slippery and wet in parts. As on other parts of Exmoor, dogs are welcomed if kept under control.

START at Anstey Gate. There are a number of ways to reach Anstey Gate, winding across the moorland roads but to pinpoint it, here's one. Head into Dulverton on the B3222 and about half a mile before the village turn left towards Hawkridge. Turn right, still towards Hawkridge and wind your way along to a T-junction. Turn left and continue on until eventually you reach Five Ways Cross (marked on signpost).

Continue along the Molland Road for about three miles, going over a cattle grid, out onto the moor, past the Hancock Memorial stone, – erected to Philip Froude Hancock an avid local huntsman on what was one of his favourite spots – and over another cattle grid. Immediately, park in the area on the left.

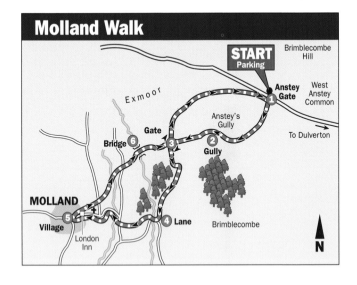

1 **Anstey Gate** – Begin the walk by heading down the clear bridleway which runs out of the car parking area, keeping the line of trees on your left. The track bears away from the trees as it goes down hill. When you come to T-junction with bank, fence and fields ahead turn right. Soon you come to a crossing track and a small farm shed.

Go up a little mound on the right and continue on in the same direction with the bank/hedge on your left. Continue downhill – the path may be a little slippery and wet and there are loose stones. It bears a little away from the bank and adjacent ditch as it continues down into Anstey's Gully.

2 **Anstey's Gully** – Cross this more open, bumpy area and stream and ascend out of the gully on the other side bearing left up a path. You reach a bank/hedge on the left and follow this all the

way until you drop down into another gully. Follow a stony path up the other side and eventually reach a gate on your left in a corner.

❸ Gate – Go through and follow the bridleway sign ahead with hedge on right. Go up to the corner of the field where another bridleway sign directs you left. Go through the gate on the right in the corner and follow a track. There are lovely views from this point as you progress, with a gully on the left, open farmland and later, a lonely Exmoor farmhouse. Follow the track all the way to the end, through a gate and out onto a lane.

❹ Lane – Turn right towards Molland. Just past a sharp left bend, ignore the bridleway sign to the right but instead follow the public footpath sign which is rather hidden behind it. This is a steep climb/scramble but short. So make your way ahead to the top where the field opens out before you. There's a stile on the far side next to a gate/opening. Cross and continue with hedge on right through a couple of gaps and out over a stile in the corner onto the road where a sign points you to Molland. Drop down and up and soon arrive in the small village.

⑤ Molland - This is a working Estate village with a unique medieval church, its own traditional village stores and post office, historic coaching inn, thatched and slate cob cottages.

The amazing 44 box pews are the first thing to capture the attention in St Mary's Church but there's much more to come. It has one of the finest collections of Georgian and protestant furnishings in Devon. Note also the unusual three-deck pulpit. The stonework of the church dates back to the fifteenth century. The font is actually 12th Century. There are a number of interesting memorials including those to the Courtenay family, and to the Quartly family who made their name as breeders of the Ruby Red breed of Devon cattle.

There's also a note about the Molland Lilly (note spelling with two ls). It is a rare plant in this country and thought to have been brought to North Devon by monks returning from a pilgrimage to Spain. Nowadays it can sometimes be seen in the hedgerows around Molland and of course, you are asked not to pick this beautiful and rare flower. The lily is carved on a chair up by the altar and remembered on some of the kneelers, too. Look for the old stocks which were in the porch when I came here.

Next door stands The London Inn, a 15th Century former coaching inn.

Over the centuries some things may have changed a little – the present bar was once the brewhouse, the family room the stables and the dining room was the original inn – but the tradition of a welcome and good food goes on.

On leaving the pub turn right up the side road. The tarmac soon gives way to a rougher surface. Go through the farm gates and pass the farmhouse on your left. Continue on into a field and here leave the track and go diagonally up right across the field as directed by the footpath sign to a gate. Having gone through, continue to climb gently up across the field and through a smaller wooden gate on the far side. Come onto a lane and cross over, going through a gate. Continue on and soon see the moor ahead.

Now aim just to the right of a split clump of trees and pick up a low grass track running down into a gully. Pass a waymark sign and continue on to another which directs you right down steps and across a double footbridge. Go steeply uphill in direction of the arrow bearing up left towards the corner of a hedge/bank. You may find a faint grassy track taking you up. Continue on to a small metal gate on the left. Go through and on to the corner of the fenced area and another waymark. Carry on in the same direction to a gate in the corner and out onto a lane.

Take the lane opposite and come down to a farm. Continue on the track past the farm and come down to a stream and concrete bridge.

⑥ Bridge – Cross and come back on to moorland, following the track which bends its way uphill to a waymark signpost and continue on up with the hedge on your right.

In the corner come to the gate that you went through on the outward leg of the walk (point 3). Don't go through this time, but instead turn left along the bank/hedge and at the corner continue straight ahead along a grassy track across the moorland. Up on the skyline on the right is a line of trees which you are paralleling. Your car is parked at the left-hand end of those trees.

Continue to walk up the track away from the gate. Take the first track right and continue on this across the moorland which may be wet in places and up towards the trees. The track bears right and starts gently to climb. At a fork, take the left hand one (more or less straight ahead) and still going uphill. Continue climbing steadily until you reach the start.

London Inn
Molland.
Call: 01769 550269

Sample the high life

Beacon Hill – Bicknoller – Beacon Hill

5.2 miles, 2.75 hours walking.

OS Explorer 22, Quantock Hills, ref: 117 410.

The Quantock Hills show their true glorious colours on this circle, starting with rhododendrons then through to gorse, heather and bronze Autumn beeches.

It is a high and open circle starting half way up and climbing steadily and quite steeply on to Beacon Hill, then along the top with fantastic views on all sides and one or two more small ascents and then drop down to pretty Bicknoller and a thatched pub. We climb some of the way up the hill after the village and then walk round the side before a steep ascent back to the start.

It's about 1.7 hours walking time to the pub but allow plenty of time to soak up the beauty of it all.

in the National Trust's Beacon Hill car park. From the A38 Bridgwater/Minehead road, at West Quantockhead (St Audries) about a mile east of Williton, turn up the lane (The Avenue) at the side of a restaurant (the Windmill), signed to Bicknoller 1.75 miles, into West Quantockhead village. At the next small crossroads and a village notice board, go steeply left up an unmarked tarmac lane, the Avenue. After the cattle grid follow the track on and up to the car park at the very end.

① Beacon Hill car park – Take the left hand of two main tracks climbing up from the car park. It's smaller than the main one. Follow it uphill through gorse and bracken with Vinney Combe down on left.

As the track starts to bend left, fork up right on grassy track. Turn round to enjoy the widespread views across to Wales and down to Minehead. After 10 minutes reach the trigpoint with views all round.

Here is a sign explaining the Beacon Hill Bronze Age Barrow here which is being restored by the National Trust. It is an ancient burial mound, one of about 30 bowl barrows on Quantock.

Take the right hand of three tracks leading away on the other side of the trig. Reach a broad crossing track. Turn right and continue on to another track, the Great Road. Go more or less straight over this, with a bit of a dog-leg.

② Bicknoller Post. – At another junction see the post over left, dated 1947 and

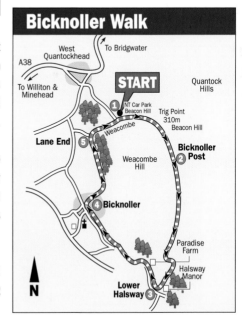

Bicknoller Walk

erected by Louis Gimblett. Continue on the main track ignoring any side paths. After about 2.5 minutes, pass a post directing vehicles to the left. Soon, just before the main track begins to curve left, reach an open grassy area on the right. Go across this and take the broad grassy track on the far side which goes uphill. Continue the steady climb to the top and after a short distance on the flat of about 25 yards, fork off to the right (second track on the right, not the one which turns at 90 degrees). It goes round the side of

the hill below the main track. There are great views over the valley to the West as you continue along here.

Stay on this path for about five minutes, ignoring a crossing track and going across the head of Paradise Combe, on the right which is wooded on one side. Eventually reach a dip – the head of Halsway Combe. Go sharp right down the clear grassy path through the bracken and then down under a line of beech trees – a familiar Quantock sight. Continue on down the side of the combe, through a stock proof gate and on down to reach the lane at Lower Halsway.

On the left is ancient Halsway Manor now the only permanent residential folk music centre in the country.

❸ **Lower Halsway** - Turn right on the lane and continue on for about six minutes to Paradise Farm where the lane becomes a track. Continue on and at Quantock Greenway post, just before a farm, follow the path ahead and continue in the Bicknoller direction. The path is sheltered and becomes stony as you

continue along and then descend. Bend left and reach a tarmac lane. Go ahead on Trendle Lane and pass along the ribbon development of country homes as you walk into Bicknoller.

Until the early 19th Century this was the main road from Taunton to Minehead.

4 Bicknoller - Reach a triangle of green and turn left down Church Lane to the church. On the green outside under the oak is a map of the village set in stone to mark the Millennium. In the churchyard admire the 1,000 year old yew under which are the village stocks. Inside are wonderfully carved bench ends and rood screen. Note the original medieval stone altar which escaped demolition by Cromwell's men.

Our walk continues right along Gatchells Lane but the friendly Bicknoller Inn is just a minute away straight on down and well worth a visit.

It was a coaching inn, dating back to the 14th Century and still has a real olde worlde feel.

Follow Gatchells Lane to another junction to the village shop and post office- an interesting project for anyone who lives in a village where their post office and shop are threatened.

After the collapse in 1991 of the Bicknoller Post Office, a project was launched to try and replace it. Of course, with only 300 people in the village, a commercially viable enterprise was out of the question. There was strong village support and three years later a limited company 'not for profit' was formed.

Interest-free loans were raised from villagers which, with a grant from the Rural Development Agency, and this enabled a derelict barn leased from the Village Hall to be renovated and kitted out.

A committee of eight supervises the Association and a team of 30 (almost 10% of the population) staff the PO/Shop on a rota basis. No wages are paid and even the Sub postmaster's fee is paid directly into the Association's account.

The Shop carries over 300 lines to supplement the fortnightly visit to the

small stream. The path climbs at first and then levels out and goes round the side of the hill. Keep on for well over half a mile always on the main track, ignoring a crossing track and also a track which forks to the right. Drop down and go through a gate and over a wooden bridge to the end of a tarmac lane by a cottage.

5 **Lane end** - Turn right. Go through a gate and straight ahead signed to Bicknoller Post going along the side of Weacombe for a short way. A track joins from the left and shortly afterwards, at a fork, go left climbing steeply up out of the combe all the way to a gate at the top into the car park.

supermarket. Wherever possible local produce is stocked and Somerset cheese and eggs are particularly popular.

The initial loans were repaid within three years and turnover remains healthy – but the real bonus has been the social impact on the village providing a regular meeting place.

Take Hill Lane straight uphill from the shop. Carry on when it becomes a track. Go through a gate onto National Trust land, Bicknoller Hill, and for a short while go ahead towards Bicknoller Combe. Then follow a green arrow left across a

Bicknoller Inn
Bicknoller.
Call: 01984 656234, open daily.

Coast to boast about

Lilstock beach – Kilve Pill – Kilve – Kilton – Kilstock Beach

6 miles. About 3 hours walking

OS Explorer 22, Quantock Hills, ref: 117 066

This is a very special coastal walk in West Somerset with the Quantocks on one side and the Severn estuary and Steep Holm on the other. A real treasure at the end is what must be one of the smallest churches in England nestling near the coast in an old graveyard full of wild flowers. There's historical interest at

Kilve Pill and a charming tea-room for lunch or refreshment, plus a popular pub at Kilve village.

The going is along a famous stretch of fossil coast on low cliffs, then on footpaths and quiet lanes and tracks with two hills – unfortunately one of them comes just after the lunch stop at Kilve village!

START in the car park for Lilstock **Beach.** This is tucked away about two miles from Kilve along narrow country lanes. From the A39 Bridgwater to Minehead road there is a bend between Kilve and Holford. Turn here on the lane to Stogursey. Stay in the Kilton direction (not Stogursey). Go through the farming hamlet of Kilton and then bend left passing Kilton church and carry on. Just past Lilstock Farm, at the bend go left on track marked as Access to Lilstock Beach. Follow this rough track to the car parking at the end.

① **Lilstock Beach car park** - From the car park continue on past a big metal gate and you will soon reach the estuary edge and Lilstock beach with incredible views across to Steep Holm, and the great contrast of Hinkley Point Power Station further up.

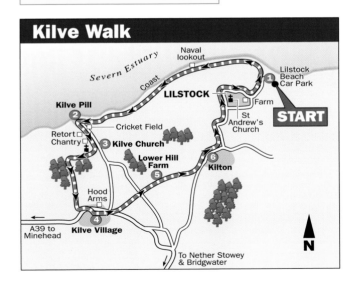

Kilve Walk

Lilstock was once a small port whose heyday was the 19th Century. Coal was brought from Wales for domestic use on the Acland estate, for the large lime kiln on the cliff and pit props were exported. There were resident coastguards, a customs officer, an inn by the beach and in about 1860 a small pier was built with a summerhouse at the end where landowner Sir Peregrine Acland used to picnic with guests. A severe storm eventually swept it away. There was apparently also a promenade along the cliff for the local gentry and in the 1860s and 70s pleasure steamers plied the coast calling in at Lilstock.

Turn left and follow this coastal path, with a great view of the Quantocks on your left and further on good views up the coast to North Hill, Minehead.

This stretch of coast is made up of exposed rock formations and fossils and it contains some of the earliest fossil ammonites found in Britain. A favourite to find is the devil's toenail!

Pass a Royal Naval Quadrant look-out hut en route and continue to Kilve Pill with the new cricket pavilion and ground where cricket can be played to the sound of the sea.

❷ Kilve Pill - You are now about 45 minutes into the walk.

Kilve Pill, like Lilstock, was once a tiny port, used for importing culm, an inferior type of coal used in the lime burning process. It is just possible to make out the remains of a stone jetty and the ruins of a lime kiln nearby where limestone was burnt to provide lime to spread on the fields. The Pill was long associated with smuggling.

Turn left on the track inland. Pass an interesting old brick retort built in the 1920s the first structure designed to convert shale into oil. The project proved to be too costly and the venture failed.

Continue inland, through the car park, and passing the Chantry Tea -Rooms where you can enjoy coffee, teas or lunches. Then come to the ruins of the old chantry.

It was was founded in 1329, when a brotherhood of five monks were employed to say Mass for their founder, Simon de Furneaux. Legend has it that barrels of spirits hidden in the chantry by smugglers were deliberately set fire to as the revenue men appeared on the scene. Whatever happened, the chantry seems to have fallen into a ruin long before the dissolution of the monasteries, and for centuries served as a barn for the farm.

❸ Kilve Church – Continue on to the church. Go into the churchyard to the main door.

The peaceful little 14th Century church of St Mary's, Kilve, was open when I came here in keeping with the welcoming notice on the door. In the vestry is a beautiful carved arch of the ancient screen and at the back of the church is an interesting photographic exhibition of the tower restoration project.

Continue along the churchyard path and out the other side into a field. Follow the marked track along the field edge heading towards woodland. Cross a small forded stream and then a stile by an opening and walk across the field. At the far side, stay in the field, turning left up the edge and climbing with woodland on the right. Take time to enjoy the views as you climb. When the woodland ends go ahead through an opening in the hedge ahead and then right through a small gate. Now go left up the left hedge, in the same direction as before, and still climbing. You get a great view across the Quantocks. Go through into another field, still along the left hedge, and dropping downhill. Just before a rather stubby oak tree, go left, down and over a stile in the hedge. Go ahead across the field, which maybe fenced off on each side as horse paddocks. Come out onto the main road and turn left. Cross with care and walk along on the other side facing traffic. After a couple of minutes, by the car park sign get off the main road on the parallel path which runs into the car park. Go out to the main road again.

④ Kilve Village - Cross and come to the Hood Arms, a 17th Century coaching inn. This part of the walk has taken about 1.5 hours.

Keep on past the village shop, cross a stream and go left at the side of the phone box along a bridleway. Now there is an eight minute steady climb up a high hedged sunken track which may be a little wet in parts.

Turn left when you reach the lane and then take Lower Hill on the right and follow it down to a farm. There are great coastal views.

⑤ Lower Hill Farm - Cross the stream with the farmhouse on your left and go ahead a few yards on a stony track and then head up the marked footpath to Kilton into a field. Follow the right hedge through two fields – in the gap between the two is a great picnic stop with far ranging views up and down the coast! Carry on and go through a metal barrier and across the end of the field to the hedge line opposite. A stile by a metal gate brings you onto a lane. You are now following on foot the route you drove to the starting car park.

⑥ Kilton - Turn left and go through Kilton hamlet. Continue on the lane, reaching on the right the medieval church of St Andrew's.

Now protected as a grade II listed building, it is a real gem, seating about 12 people only and one of the most atmospheric settings I have ever seen. St Andrew's still manages one service a year. When I came in mid May the old much weathered gravestones were cocooned in drifts of wild flowers.

To finish the walk follow the lane past Lilstock Farm and turn left on the track to the car park.

Chantry tea-rooms
Kilve beach, are open all year.
Call: 01278 741457
Hood Arms
Kilve.
Call: 01278 741210

Marsh lair of the king

Burrow Mump – Athelney – East Lyng – Burrow Mump

5.5 miles. 3 hours walking

OS Explorer 22, Quantock Hills and Bridgwater, ref: 360 307

The Isle of Athelney, now just a very slight incline
on the Levels between Taunton and Glastonbury,
was once the fortified island from which King Alfred
launched successful attacks against the Danes.
This very easy circle takes us on a visit to the look-out
where Alfred kept an eye on the Danes and past
a Monument to Alfred near the site of Athelney Abbey.
The walk starts with a short steep climb up lofty
Burrow Mump and then follows the River Parrett
Trail to Athelney where a lane takes us on to East Lyng.
Follow an ancient drove across the Levels followed
by about two miles on quiet tarmac lanes. There are
no hills, except for the Mump and it's good at any
time of year, likely to be dry underfoot most of
the way. Refreshment can be taken at East Lyng
or at the King Alfred Inn at the foot of the Mump.
It's also a good walk for bird watching as the area
is a favourite over-wintering place for many species.
You may also glimpse water voles and otters.

START at the **National Trust car park at the foot of the mound of Burrow Mump at Burrowbridge.** The village lies on the A361 between Taunton and Glastonbury. The Mump car park is on the Glastonbury side of the village.

① **Burrow Mump** – The Mump may have been used as a look-out for King Alfred during his campaigns against the Danes. The ruined chapel at the top belonged to Athelney Abbey and during the Civil War was occupied by Royalist troops and later captured for the Parliament. The Chapel at the top dates back to the 12th Century. It was severely damaged after the Battle of Langport and although rebuilding began it was never finished.

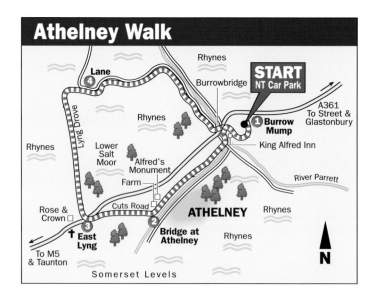

Athelney Walk

Climb up to the ruins at the top and enjoy the tremendous views and then go over the other side, bearing right down to a wooden hunting gate in the corner. Then it's down steps to the road. Turn left and pass the King Alfred Inn (ignore the path at the side). After crossing the bridge over the River Parrett, immediately turn left by the phone box on a small path alongside the river – the Macmillan Trail.

The Parrett, which was tidal up to Burrowbridge, used to be a busy thoroughfare for goods, such as withies, Roman tiles, hides and ciders on large specially designed barges.

Follow the path with the river on the left – in one part it is rather uneven – and reach a road. Go straight over on the Parrett Trail, which at this point follows the River Tone, not the Parrett! The trail is 47 miles long crossing Somerset and Dorset. Continue along the trail with the river on your left for over a mile going through stiles and gates en route. Ahead you can see King Alfred's Monument. Begin to get close to the small hamlet of Athelney with houses over on the other side of the river. See a very large red brick farm ahead on the right. The Monument is on a small hill in a field behind. Come to a stile/metal gate (with another shortly ahead).

If you want to visit Alfred's monument it's a very short detour: don't cross the stile, but turn right down the fence line. At the end go left through a gate and shortly right over a rhyne and through another gate and follow the farmhouse house wall on your left up to Alfred's Monument. It's only a few minutes.

The monument was built by John Slade who owned the site here where Athelney Abbey used to be. He erected it to commemorate Alfred's time in the area.

Retrace your steps to the gate by the river, making sure you close all gates behind you.

Go over the stile by the gate and then do the same at another gate to reach a lane by a bridge at Athelney.

Athelney, which means 'noble island', was fortified by King Alfred as a base to launch attacks against the Danes. He eventually forced them out of Wessex and later out of the whole of Southern England and in thanks Alfred returned to Athelney and founded a vast Benedictine abbey. Nothing remains of the building but it has been excavated and was the subject of two BBC Time Team programmes. Various relics have been found including a gold necklet inscribed with the words "Alfred had me wrought" which is housed in the Ashmolean museum, Oxford.

2 **Bridge at Athelney** – There is an information board about Stanmoor Bank flood defence scheme. Go right on the quiet lane, looking across withy beds, reminding us that willow production is still a flourishing industry on the Levels. After just over half a mile the lane goes along a raised wall, also part of flood defences, and comes into the village of East Lyng.

3 **East Lyng** – Turn left on the main road. Cross and go right down Hectors Lane. The church a little further along the main road on the left has an interesting stained glass window of Alfred. The welcoming Rose and Crown is also just along the road if you need refreshment at this stage.

Follow Hector's Lane which eventually turns into a drove across the Levels. The next mile and a half is a quiet flat progress across this area, known as Higher Salt Moor where cattle graze peacefully. At a T-junction with another drove, turn right and soon come to a lane.

4 **Lane** – Turn right and after a mile reach a T-junction. Turn right and follow the road alongside the River Parrett which is up over the bank on the left.

Pass attractive red brick farms and homes spread out on the edge of Burrowbridge and ignore any side tracks. After about three quarters of a mile come to the main road at Burrowbridge and turn left over the bridge back to the King Alfred Inn. To reach the car park, turn left along the road or retrace your steps over the Mump.

King Alfred Inn
Call: 01823 698379
Only open Fridays-Sundays during the Winter, and open daily after Easter.

The Rose and Crown
East Lyng.
Call: 01823 698235
open for lunch daily.

Wardour Castle Walk

**Old Wardour Castle – Wardour Castle –
Donhead St Andrew – Old Wardour Castle.**

About 4.75 miles, approx 2.5 hours walking.

OS Explorer 118 Shaftesbury & Cranbourne Chase. Ref: 938 263

A truly magical circle which visits two castles – one a
romantic ruin and the other a large and imposing
Palladian style mansion both surrounded by gardens
and parkland much of which was the work of
Capability Brown. The setting is the glorious well
wooded limestone country of South West Wiltshire
not far from Shaftesbury. We walk through a beautiful
valley where the rivers Wylye and Nadder flow,
bounded by Salisbury Plain in the north and
Cranbourne Chase south. It's an area of combes and
hills, hidden tracks and lanes sprinkled with lovely
villages and we have the added bonus of spending
quite a bit of time in the parklike estate of the
two castles. A wonderful any season walk.
Walking is on tracks and lanes and even through
the fields you are unlikely to encounter much
wet or mud.

START at **Old Wardour Castle which is East of Shaftesbury and north of the A30. Follow the signs along lanes and a drive to the castle and into the car park.**

❶ Old Wardour Castle – Old Wardour Castle in an idyllic setting beside a lake, and surrounded by the gentle Wiltshire countryside, typifies the idea of a 'romantic ruin'.

It was built, not as a powerful fortress, but along the lines of a comfortable residence

with the means to provide lavish entertaining and accommodation for guests. In 1393 Lord Lovel, with the help of a great medieval architect, began to create the unique design of Old Wardour Castle. As a veteran of the Hundred Years War, Lord Lovel may have been inspired by the chateaux in France, but certainly his castle was unparalleled in the whole of England. Based on a hexagonal plan, Old Wardour has flanking towers to the entrance, and a small hexagonal courtyard in the centre of the building containing a well. It is made of locally quarried Tisbury greensand. No expense was spared and it must have

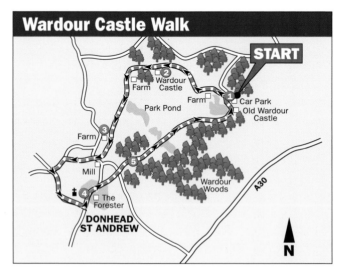

Wardour Castle Walk

proved Lord Lovel with a comfortable and secure home in his retirement. But turbulent times, and changing fortunes lead to its demise. When Lovel's great grandson lost the family's estate in 1460, there followed a rapid succession of owners and tenants until it was eventually purchased by Sir Matthew Arundell in 1570 and was remodelled and modernised. Following many skirmishes between the Royalists and the Parliamentarians during the Civil War, and a four-month long bombardment, the old castle suffered severe damage. It was virtually destroyed, and later abandoned and is now a ruin with arches, rooms and staircases that lead nowhere and a rocky grotto.

The castle is cared for by English Heritage and a must for a visit, with a very modest charge which includes the use of a very good audio guide. On a practical note, teas and coffees can be obtained from the entrance kiosk and there are toilets.

From the car park, cross the entrance drive and take the drive on the other side going away from the castle with a pond on your left (As you approach the car park the drive is on the right). This is the Wessex Ridgeway long distance path.

Follow this along and through Ark Farm going between the barns and on as it bends towards the impressive 'new' castle built to replace the old ruined castle which was beyond repair. Shortly when the track bends left, go right over a marked stile and follow this track with the fence on your right towards the new castle.

2 New Wardour Castle – This replacement 'castle' for Old Wardour was built in the 18th Century by the 8th Lord Arundel of Wardour and is set in beautiful gardens and estate with a series of ponds, much of it the work of Capability Brown and only just completed before he died.

Cross a stile into the grounds and follow the drive along the back of the building which is now converted into luxury apartments.

There is an interesting catholic chapel but it is closed except for Sunday services. There used to be a very big catholic community in the area.

Pass the house and immediately turn left round the end into an open space known as the Chapel Garden. Pass close to the left of the new building and then pick up a track through a band of woodland to a stile. You are no longer on the Wessex Ridgeway.

(NB: At the time of writing, discussions were taking place about re-routing the footpath. This would push it away from the house. If this happens, it will be well signed and where the path crosses the drive you are likely to be directed left off the Wessex Ridgeway, towards the right of the new building and on to the stile.)

Cross the stile into a field. Go down across the field, enjoying this glorious park-like countryside, and heading towards the right of the house below you.

Cross a stile; go straight over the track and over another stile. Pass to the right side of the farmhouse and head to the far side of the field. Go through gate and cross the stream. Continue on in the same direction heading towards the right side of woodland. Cross two stiles close together and continue on with the trees on the left.

Up on the left above the bank is one of the ponds of the estate.

Carry on, heading towards a farm on the far side of the field. Reach a hunting gate at the end marked with a footpath arrow. Go along with a laurel hedge and farmhouse garden on the right. Go through the farmyard onto a track. Take the stile ahead on the other side of the track and head up the field to the far end. Leave by a stile to the left of the metal six bar gate. A short grassy track leads to the lane.

❸ Lane – Turn right passing a converted mill house on your right. Go on a few more yards across a short bridge and immediately turn left over a wooden stile fence. Go on across rough land to two more stiles and into a field. This is the first real uphill of the day – climb straight up the field to the top. Go through a metal gate and cross the narrow field ahead to go through another gate onto a lane.

Turn left and follow the lane uphill to a junction. Turn left passing Beauchamp House and a number of other attractive country homes. You are dropping downhill now into the attractive hamlet of Donhead St Andrew.

④ Donhead St Andrew – Carry on past the church and up to a junction with the Tisbury/Shaftesbury road. Turn left and walk into the main part of this hamlet to the welcoming Forester inn – a great place for refreshment.

Carry on through the village for a little longer and fork right into Wardour Lane. Follow it uphill past cottages. At the junction go straight ahead up the No Through Road, passing a number of beautiful homes. At the end go into Wardour Wood, managed by Forest Enterprise.

⑤ Wood – Follow the main broad track which as you get near the top, gently bends down left and then bears away right. The track continues on along through the edge of the woodland, but don't carry on along this. Instead, almost immediately, you turn left on a track and then after a couple of yards turn right along a small path down to a gate at the edge of the wood.

Cross a stile by a gate marked with the Wessex Ridgeway sign and go ahead across the field towards a pond. Cross a stile and go through the woodland with a pond on the right and a stream and remains of a pond on your left.

Leave the wood over a stile by an opening and follow the left fence in the field uphill. Great views over new Wardour Castle unfold as you continue. Cross a stile and carry on in the same direction as before along a track along the edge of woodland. Before too long the old Castle comes into view, a memorable sight with the stone ruins, beautiful grounds and backcloth of magnificent woodland.

Follow the track all the way back to the old castle and the start.

The Forester
Donhead St Andrew.
Call: 01747 828038

At the gates of heaven

**Nockatt Coppice – Heaven's Gate - Longleat park – Crockerton –
Shear Water – Nockatt Coppice**

About 7.25 miles, or 6.25 miles without visiting the village and pub.

Explorer OS map 143, Warminster & Trowbridge, ref 828 423

The Longleat Estate near Warminster is a beautiful
landscaped English 'paradise' which welcomes sensible
walkers and visitors. We stride out to Heaven's Gate
ridge with an unrivalled view over the estate and house
and then follow the hill before dropping down to walk
through the estate along the entrance drive flanked by
breathtaking azaleas, rhododendrons and glorious
trees. After following a quiet lane, we go through a
pretty village to a very special country pub. And it's not
over yet! The walk then goes to the beauty spot of
Shear Water and on into dappled pine woods.
There's the chance of a cup of tea at Shear Water,
too. It's easy walking, mainly on the flat, on dry tracks
and lanes and ideal for all seasons including winter
when the views and the trees will be more starkly
dramatic. Spring brings bluebells and wild flowers
and late Spring and early summer, the best time
of all, sees a riot of azaleas and rhododendrons in
the park and in the adjoining woods. Autumn brings

spectacular orange and golden hues. There may be some traffic along the Estate entrance drive but it's along here that you see the rhododendrons and magnificent trees at their best. Dogs must be kept on a lead through the estate and under control at all times.

START at Nockatt Coppice car park: from the A362 Frome to Warminster road on the outskirts of Warminster go to Picket Post Gate roundabout near Longleat entrance. Then follow the Horningsham road through the forest for about 1.5 miles to the car park along on the left.

1 **Nockatt Coppice** – Cross the road and take the track opposite into the forest, going under a magnificent copper beech tree almost immediately. Follow the path along between gorgeous trees and a wonderful array of azaleas and rhododendrons. Go through a double wooden gate and reach Heaven's Gate.

This superb viewpoint is now crowned by dramatic stone sculptures, marking the new Millennium. This vantage point amongst the beeches on the hill was designed by Capability Brown when he drew up plans for the whole estate. There are benches for you to sit and enjoy the vista over Longleat House and estate.

The present house, built in the second half of the 16th Century by Sir John Thynn, on

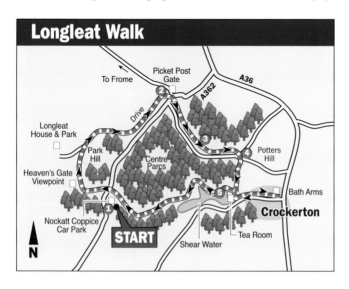

Turn right uphill along the side of the road, where in the summer at weekends you may encounter traffic. Further on, there is room for you to walk on the broad verge at the side. Pass the entrance booths and keep on and then shortly turn left alongside the no through drive.

the site of a medieval priory of the Black Canons, is considered to be one of the best examples of high Elizabethan architecture in the country. It is set in 900 acres of magnificent parkland, much of it designed by Capability Brown. The present owner, the 7th Marquis of Bath, Alexander Thynn is a descendant of Sir John. It was the first stately home to open its doors to the public in 1949 and is still one of the top attractions in Britain, with house, safari park, mazes and other amusements.

Turn right along the track along the ridge which soon becomes a good tarmac drive.

From here you may be able to get glimpses of the safari park.

After going through a wooden barrier reaches the entrance drive to Longleat.

It's along here that the rhododendrons and azaleas are absolutely magnificent with their scent pervading the air.

❷ End of drive – After just over half a mile reach the end of the drive, just before the Picket Post roundabout.

Turn right on the Horningsham road and shortly, take the first left and follow this quiet and pretty lane through the forest for about 1.5 miles.

Along here, azaleas and rhododendrons have escaped to give us vivid glimpses of yellow and mauve in late Spring.

❸ Footpath – Ignore a left turn and not long after, when you reach a crossing footpath, turn right. It was rather churned up when I walked here, due to forestry operations, but there was no real problem. Follow it downhill through a bluebell wood. Stay on the path which gently bends right and continues to descend, ignoring a track going right.

4 **Lane** - Reach a lane on the edge of Potter's Hill. Here there is a choice: First the main route through Potter's Hill and adjoining Crockerton and a visit to the pub. Secondly the short route back omitting village and pub.

1 To continue the main route, turn left and come into the village, passing the village school.

You will notice the unusual church tower up on the left, but this is no longer a church – it was converted into a private house in the 1990s.

Just past the school, turn right down Broadmead Lane and Potter's Hill and follow the lane downhill, passing a variety of pretty cottages, crossing a small stream at the bottom and then climb more gently up the other side.

At the junction at the top in Crockerton, turn left for a couple of minutes to the popular Bath Arms which has a very good menu and seating options outside.

Retrace your steps to the top of Broadmead Lane from where you have just come and then continue on. Turn right down a small lane which runs along by pretty cottages below the village road you were on. Then at the junction at the end turn left back up to the road and turn right. It was just a short detour which is prettier than the upper road!

Reach Broadmead Lane and turn right down hill. At the sharp right corner, go left on the footpath into the woods and continue on.

❷ For the short option, turn right and at the sharp left corner, go ahead on the footpath into woods and continue on.

Soon both paths come to the boat park for Shear Water Sailing Club and then to the end of the lake itself.

❺ **Shear Water lake** – This beautiful spot is a mecca for fishermen, sailors, those who just want a tranquil rest by the water, and like the rest of the Longleat estate is beautifully maintained.

For refreshment, turn left along the path along the dam and reach the restaurant and tea rooms at the end.

To continue our circle, follow the tarmac drive with the lake on your left. Keep straight on through a wooden barrier (just beyond this there's a great picnic bench by the lake!) and shortly turn left following the wooden signpost to Nockatt Coppice car park. It's a dry stony track through the pine and bluebell woods. After about three quarters of a mile, reach a junction of tracks and turn right. Come up to a T-junction of tracks at the edge of the forest, and turn right and the track brings you back to the start.

Bath Arms
Crockerton.
Call: 01985 212262

From Wansdyke to canal

Walkers Hill car park − All Cannings − Alton Barnes − Walkers Hill

8 miles, 4.5 hours walking

OS Explorer 157, Marlborough & Savernake Forest, ref: 115 637

Try this wonderful Autumn bracer near Pewsey if you want to experience the wide open downland of Wiltshire and then the contrast of a flat canal towpath walk. It's also great if you are at all interested in crop circles as we pass the Barge Inn on the canal at Honeystreet, an internationally renowned crop circle venue. The first part of the walk follows the ancient Saxon earthwork, the Wansdyke, along which a long distance path is being developed. As we start high up, this means a steep uphill climb at the end, so conserve some of your energy! Well-controlled dogs can have a great time on this circle, too.

START at **Walkers Hill car park, 8 miles South West of Marlborough and between Devizes and Pewsey.** It is on the road between Fyfield on the A4 near Avebury and Alton Barnes. If coming from Fyfield in the North it is about 4.4 miles and on your left.

① **Walkers Hill car park** - Cross the road to an English Heritage sign about archaeological sites at New Town Farm and go over the stile and follow the track uphill for a good half mile. Start to descend a little and ignore the footpath on the left; continue a few yards to a gate and another stile on your left. Cross this onto the grassy track which is the Wansdyke Path.

This defensive earthwork, one of the largest in the UK, dates back to the Dark Ages, probably from the 5th Century and

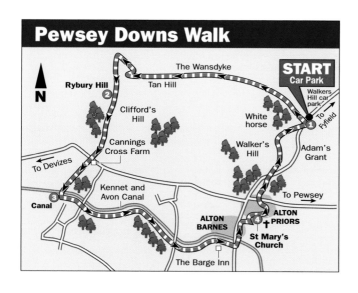

Pewsey Downs Walk

runs from the Avon valley south of Bristol to Savernake Forest near Marlborough in Wiltshire. Wansdyke was originally a large bank with a deep ditch in front, running east-west, presumably as a defence against danger from the north. A long-term aim is to complete a footpath all along the Wansdyke. This section in the East has for some time been accessed by the beautiful Wansdyke Path. The hope is to extend it westward towards Bath and then on to Bristol, not only to preserve this unique monument but also to benefit walkers.

Follow the Wansdyke for about two miles, crossing a track on the way. It's exhilarating walking with incredible views, sweeping downland fields and maybe a few hang-gliders to keep you company. Pass on the left Tan Hill, the highest point in Wiltshire.

The views are breathtaking, looking across to the Cotswolds and Mendips in the northwest and southwest, respectively, across the Vale of Pewsey to Salisbury Plain in the south, along the escarpment to the east and up to Silbury Hill, Avebury and the Marlborough Downs to the north.

Reach a point where you have to drop down off the Wansdyke – there's a stile and waymarked gate down on the right. Ignore these and instead look up left to a white arrow on the fence above. Go up here and follow the grassy track away from the Wansdyke now with the fence on your right.

❷ **Rybury Hill Camp** - Cross a stile into Tan Hill, Clifford's Hill and Rybury Hill Camp Iron Age hillfort and follow the grassy track dropping downhill. Pass a small concrete reservoir on the right and shortly go through a gate. Take the grassy path which goes round the right side of Rybury Hill. This is open access land so you can climb up to the top of Rybury Hill if you wish.

Follow the path all the way to the main road and cross over to Cannings Cross Farm. Go through the farm keeping the farmhouse on your left and follow the track out the other side. As the track bends left, go straight ahead across the field on a grassy swathe and rather surprisingly reach the Kennet & Avon Canal.

❸ Canal – Cross the canal and go down left onto the towpath which you now follow for about 2.5 miles. You soon see the Alton Barnes White Horse up on the hill on the left.

This is one of eight Wiltshire White Horses and was cut in 1812. It looks westwards towards the latest horse, the Millennium White Horse above Devizes. The foreman who designed it absconded with his £20 advance and was later hanged for sheep stealing.

The welcome sight of the Barge Inn comes into view.

It is not just a beautifully sited pub, but is also considered to be one of the leading centres internationally for crop circle

enthusiasts. Inside there are amazing photographs of crop circles and much interesting information. The Barge Inn opened in 1810 to cater for the busy trade on the newly opened canal.

Continue along the towpath and leave it at the next bridge. Go up, cross the bridge and follow the road for about six minutes. Turn right towards St Mary's Saxon Church in Alton Priors.

4 St Mary's Church – It's worth visiting this beautiful little Anglo Saxon church at the end. Just before the church go through the wooden roundabout stile and follow the brick path across the field and then go right with the back of the church over on your right. Go through a roundabout stile into another field and follow the path to another church.

All Saints, this one is no longer used for services and has a rather neglected and sad air. In the churchyard to the south of the church is a yew tree said to be 1,700 years old.

From the church carry on for a few yards in the same direction as before and then turn left across the field. Just before you reach the corner of the long thatched wall – go diagonally left across the field to the left side and cross a stile onto a lane. Turn right and go up to the junction with the road.

Cross and take the footpath opposite. Go up the right fence in the field and go round the corner a yard or two and then head across the field following the footpath sign. Go through an opening and look for the very steep path which drops down to the road – a difficult drop so take care.

Follow the marked footpath opposite which starts the uphill climb. Go through the kissing gate by the information board and go ahead up the grassy track, still ascending. Up on your right is the steep hill of Adams Grave, a prehistoric chambered long barrow in which skeletons and arrowheads were discovered. Continue on in the same direction, keeping Walkers Hill up on your left. Cross marked stiles and come out onto the road just before the car park.

The Barge Inn
Honeystreet, Pewsey.
Call: 01672 851705

Death of a Cavalier

Upper Swainswick – Langridge – Lansdown –
Woolley – Upper Swainswick

6.3 miles. About 3.50 hours walking

OS Explorer 155 Bristol & Bath, ref: 757 682

The beauty of the countryside near Bath is revealed to its full as we explore the folds, fields, dips and heights of the very quiet, sheltered and still undiscovered area to the north between Swainswick and Lansdown.

There are flower meadows, views and undulations – don't be surprised that this walk has quite a few uphill stretches as well as flats and dips. There were wild flowers including orchids everywhere when I came at the end of June and butterflies of all kinds and the air was full of bird song. En route we visit the site of a famous Civil War battle and monument to the Commander who fell there, and also stop at a renowned inn up on Lansdown. To add to that are three tucked away country churches.

START in the village of Upper **Swainswick which lies just off the A46 a couple of miles to the north of Bath**. It can also be approached from the Weston, Lansdown, Langridge direction. Park somewhere suitable in the centre of the village near a small triangle of grass with a large oak at the centre. There was a reasonable amount of safe road parking along here.

① Upper Swainswick – From the triangle of grass, walk on through the beautiful village on the main lane going slightly downhill.

Near the triangle, note the interesting old watercourse diverted out of the wall. Already there are great views across the valley.

Pass a house, Upper Westwood, and shortly go left through a gate on the public footpath. Head down the meadow to the bottom right corner by the stream, the Lam Brook, and leave over a stile onto the bridge. Turn left over the bridge and follow the lane as it winds steeply uphill.

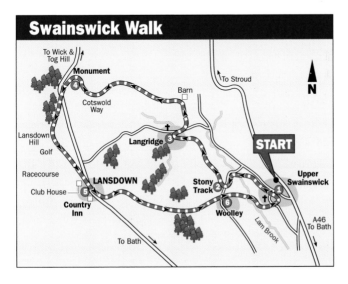

Swainswick Walk

2 **Stony track** – As you reach the top of the hill, on the edge of Woolley village, turn right on the stony track marked as a footpath. Shortly go through a gate into a field and follow the left hedge along the edge of the hill with the whole valley spread out to your right. Go through a gate in the corner and carry on along the left hedge. Cross a stile and continue straight ahead in the next field. Cross another stile and carry on as before passing a line of bushes on the right and then the field opens out. Head for the far left corner. Cross the stile and go left in the field to another stile. Once over, go ahead in the field on the ridge heading towards the small church of Langridge on the side of the hill. Follow the ridge round and then drop down to the bottom left corner just to the left of some corrugated sheds and hen houses. In the corner go over a footbridge and turn right and a stile brings you onto the lane in the tiny hamlet of Langridge

3 **Langridge** – Turn right to continue the walk but it's worth a small detour of a couple of minutes left up to the church.

St Mary the Magdalene church is a glorious little country church with an outstanding Norman arch and chancel. Above the arch is a beautiful primitive stone sculpture of the Madonna and child, probably 13th Century.

Retrace your steps and continue on the lane past the stile you have just crossed. Soon take the first tarmac lane/track left. It climbs steeply at first and then more gently. At a stone barn turn left on the marked bridleway soon going through a gate. You now have about a ten minute gentle steady climb between hedges up onto Lansdown Hill with occasional views at gate openings. You pass a stile on the right where the Cotswold Way comes and joins our route. Continue on. After a few minutes go through a gate and along the top of a field which drops away left into the valley. Head up right to the wall on the top and look for steps and a slab stile. Cross this to reach the first of several Pennants marking the site of the Civil War Battle of Lansdown on July 5, 1643. You will soon learn more about this!

Follow the wall ahead keeping it on your right and at the far side of the field go through into woodland and a dry stony path leads you through and out the other side to a Monument.

④ Monument - This was erected in memory of Sir Bevil Grenville who acquitted himself so nobly at the Battle of Lansdown as part of the Royalist force, but who died in the fighting. It was a bloody confrontation by all accounts in which the Royalists gained Lansdown Hill and eventually beat back the Parliamentarian force who retreated to Bath.

"...the air was so darkened by the smoke of the powder, that for a quarter of an hour... there was no light seen, but what the fire of the volleys of shot gave..." A description of the battle in 'The Vindication of Richard Atkyns', Peter Young.

With your back to the monument walk away from it on a path across grass which when I came at the end of June was studded with early purple orchids. At the main road, cross with care and turn left. After about a minute turn right on the tarmac track marked as a bridleway. At a barrier and gate, turn right onto a path which runs under a line of trees.

At the end reach the edge of Lansdown Hill Golf Course. Turn left on the bridleway with a wall on left and golf course on the right, keeping an eye out for golf balls. On the far side of the golf course you can see the stands of Bath Racecourse. At a crossing drive go straight over following the footpath arrow and keeping close to a line of conifers with black and white marker posts on your left. Don't stray over to the left as this area is used for golf practice. Reach the clubhouse. Walk in front of it and to the far side of the car park.

⑤ **Country Inn** - Go out onto the road and turn right to reach the Blathwayt Country Inn next door, a fine pub with a good garden, serving food every lunch-time.

Cross the main road from the pub and turn right in front of a line of cottages. Continue on past the cottages on the grassy verge and turn left on a drive over a cattle grid. Immediately go right on the footpath diagonally across the field (the sign was broken). Head for a power pole in the field, marked with a yellow arrow. Pass just to the left of it and continue on across the field bearing slightly left. Cross

over into a recreation field and go ahead parallel with the left wall with views over the Swainswick valley again. Cross a broken stone slab stile near the left corner and continue along the left wall of this field. Cross a stile to reach a farm where a lot of old cars are kept. Turn right and after a few yards, just before the farmhouse, turn left on the marked path between hedges. Go ahead in the next three fields. In the third field head towards the far side towards the far right corner. A few yards to the left of the corner ahead of you go through a way marked wooden kissing gate and descend steps. At the bottom go straight on down the field towards the valley, quite steeply, enjoying what was a meadow full of wild flowers when I came here. Don't enter the wood ahead, but instead bear left and when you can, work your way down to the right, staying in the open. Cross a stile and go along a path descending to a well appointed bench with a great valley view. Follow the path as it wends its way down and over a stile. You are descending gradually, contouring and then head for a chalet bungalow down below on the edge of Woolley. There is a stile in the fence in front of the bungalow. Cross and turn right down the tarmac drive to the road on the edge of Woolley.

⑥ Woolley – Turn left and then right down the tarmac lane by the village noticeboard to the church.

The distinctive little church of All Saints was designed by prominent Architect John Wood the Younger of Bath, dedicated in 1761.

Cross the slab stile by the side of the church and go down the path at the side. At the end, cross a stile into a field. Go ahead following the left fence and into another field still along the fence. Half way down, bear right across and down to the far corner. Cross the footbridge and turn right alongside the stream. In the corner, cross another footbridge. Now follows a steep climb left up the field heading to the right hand end of the three gable roofs. In the top edge go up steps and through a wicket gate into a cottage garden and on up more steps through the garden (Woodbine Cottage), coming out at the top onto the lane. Our way continues

straight ahead up the hill, but you may like to turn left for a visit to yet another beautiful church. There is a simple booklet giving an insight into the church's interesting history. On the way up ignore the turn to Tadwick. Just continue to the top and then turn right back to where you parked.

Blathwayt Country Inn
Call: 01225 421995

Go with the flow

Keynsham − Queen Charlton − Compton Dando − Keynsham

7.25 miles, 4 hours walking.

OS map Explorer map 155, Bristol & Bath ref: 657 683

Keynsham, between Bath and Bristol, is poised on the edge of beautiful countryside and this circle enjoys the combes, streams and views to the full, following the Two Rivers Way for much of the time. It starts by cutting along the southern edge of Keynsham, taking in a new wood and then drops down and up into quiet Queen Charlton. From there it brushes Woollard and continues through fields and a stunning bluebell wood to Compton Dando, the River Chew and a welcoming pub. From here it is easy − following the river back to Keynsham.

Walking is easy with no steep hills and has the advantage of many kissing gates and few stiles.

START in Keynsham and head down the High Street (**B3116**), away from the big church towards the large modern clock and then follow the All Routes sign down left in Bath Hill. Cross the river and at the mini roundabout turn right into Bath Hill East Car Park.

❶ Bath Hill East car park - Take the path from the car park just to the side of the first pay machine on the right. Cross the river and turn left in Keynsham Memorial Park.

The park is a small reminder of the beautiful wooded area that Keynsham once was. Indeed it was the beauty and tranquillity that, according to legend, brought Keyna the beautiful virgin daughter of an ancient Welsh prince to seek a life of peace and contemplation here. She was warned that serpents in the area would make her life

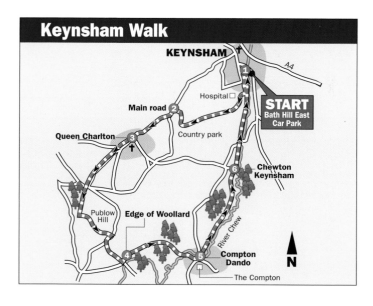

Keynsham Walk

impossible, but her powers of prayer converted them into stones. The origin of the legend may be the many fossil ammonites shaped like coiled snakes that have been dug up in the area. But it is after Keyna that the town, one of the largest conurbations in the region, is named.

Follow the river on your left, and then a duck pond and stay on the main path. Come out onto a small lane by cottages and then turn right to reach a triangle of grass with an old lamppost. Turn left and follow the lane as it climbs uphill.

Pass the hospital and already you can feel the real countryside with good views over the valley on your left. Follow this small lane and run into a more substantial road. Continue on in St Clements Road. At the end of St Clements Court take the cycleway ahead. When it ends by the entrance to an allotment, turn right in a residential road and then take Dunster Road on the left. At the bend, follow the public footpath on. It goes up to the school and then left round the edge and leads into a field. Turn right, with school over on right, and leave the field over wooden barriers on the right. Keep on through rough ground,

keeping over on the right by the houses. Cross a stile and take the tarmac path along the ends of gardens and reach Abbots Wood.

It is part of a network of community woods and was acquired by the Woodland Trust and planted in 1995.

Go right along the top of the area with houses on right and on into another section. Go diagonally left across the centre heading for an opening on the far side. Go through into another recreational area and here turn right and head over towards houses, passing a children's play park on the left. Go through a barrier into a residential area, and straight ahead by garages. At the junction turn left. At Walnut Walk and Lilac Court go ahead on the pavement to a main road.

2 Main road – Turn left and cross, and by the restriction signs, go right on the public footpath. Take the stile at the end and drop down the left side of the next field into the valley. Cross a stream on a concrete bridge and enter a field and go uphill towards Queen Charlton. A kissing

gate brings you onto a drive which leads ahead to the green at Queen Charlton, a very pretty olde-worlde spot.

3 Queen Charlton – There's a welcoming seat on the green under an old oak. I tried to visit the church but sadly found it locked. Follow the road keeping the church on your left and leave the village. Take the first turn left and immediately fork right and stay on this quiet thoroughfare for over half a mile to a fairly busy road.

Cross with caution and go down Ringspit Lane opposite. Follow the public footpath sign left over a stile and go down the track for a short way and then right through an opening into a field which may be rather overgrown. Go downhill down the left side, cross a stile and on down through a rather wild area. Look for a marked stile ahead – watch your footing – which leads to another field. Continue descending through fields along the left hedge until you cross a stile in a corner and reach a junction of paths and a footpath marker. Go left and cross the stile leads into a field. Follow the small stream on your right. Stay in the field to a stile and footbridge ahead on the far side (don't go right) and continue on following the right hedge. Cross a stile then wiggle left and right and continue on in the same direction as before along the right edge.

Up on your left is Publow Hill. Follow the hedge to the end and go over a rather awkward metal barrier gate (unmarked) and continue on down, over a stile and down steps to the lane.

Turn right. Ignore the turning on the right. Just stay on the lower lane which leads down to Woollard.

④ **Edge of Woollard** – Pass the Woollard sign and look for the Two Rivers Way footpath pointing left up a track alongside a farm. Go to the end into a field and follow the yellow Forest of Avon Community Walk signs across the field and then steeply up. Go through a kissing gate at the top and on across the field to the far side. Go through into the next field and across through another gate and on as before. On the far side of this field look for a large wooden kissing gate ahead (slightly right) leading into woods. The path drops down through this area which is a marvellous spot for bluebells in the spring. Go out into a field and go left across the field and then over a substantial metal footbridge over the River Chew. Head for the church and village of Compton Dando. Pass two unusual wagon wheel type seats by the river. Don't cross the bridge but instead follow the arrows through the farm/stables and into the churchyard. Continue on into Compton Dando.

⑤ **Compton Dando** – You can't fail to miss the Compton Inn opposite which serves food every day. Turn left on the road (turn right from the pub). After crossing the river, turn right through a gate on the Two Rivers Walk. Go ahead down the length of the field with river meandering on right. A hunting gate at the end leads to another field. Keep on along the right edge all the way to another

6 **Chewton Keynsham** – You are on the edge of the small hamlet of Chewton Keynsham (over on the left). Cross the track and follow the Two Rivers ahead across the end of a field. Go through two gates and ahead on a permissive path still following the river. Come out onto a lane and turn right.

At a bend take the hunting gate on the left and stay in this field on the flat keeping the river on the right. Continue to follow the footpath and river through fields until you reach a large old converted mill property. Follow the arrows through sticking firmly to the route.

Continue ahead past cottages on the edge of Keynsham and reach a small triangle of grass with a lamp post, where you were earlier. Turn right and left and retrace your steps back through the park to the car park.

The Compton Inn
Call: 01761 490321
Closed Monday lunch

gate and continue on in the next field, river still on right. Just before you reach woodland, branch up left onto a grass track and follow this along and into woodland, marked with the Two Rivers sign. You are higher than the river now, but still following its course. Go through a hunting gate out of a wood and follow the path along the right of the field. Yet another gate awaits you and then go up onto a bit of a ridge in the field. Go through another hunting gate and head across to another gate where you can see the path has been officially rerouted. So go along the right edge by the river and on into another field and again on following the river. A gate leads to a track.

Monumental but short

North Nibley – Pitt Court – Tyndale Monument – North Nibley

4.3 miles, 2 hours walking.

OS map Explorer map 167, Thornbury, Dursley & Yate ref: 740 958

Short on time, but not short on beauty, this is a good walk for a morning or afternoon in South Gloucestershire on the edge of the Cotswolds escarpment. Start in North Nibley and take a footpath to the quiet hamlet of Pitt Court and follow narrow country lanes, with the backdrop of a Cotswold wooded hill, to climb gently up onto the Cotswold escarpment.

Then there is the contrast of walking through mixed woodland before emerging up onto open land with breath-taking views and coming to the 130 ft high stone tower that is such a prominent landmark, Tyndale Monument. It's an ideal all the year round circle with the very popular Black Horse Inn serving excellent food at the end in North Nibley. There is also the option of a short diversion at Waterley Bottom to the New Inn. It is a steady climb up to the Cotswold wooded top, but nothing very steep, and after the Monument, comes a steep, stepped drop down on the Cotswold Way but there are no very steep uphill stretches. There are few stiles – mainly kissing gates. Dogs will have a good time, but they are not allowed in the pub.

North Nibley : **WALK 14**

If coming the short route you will go through Nibley Green which is the site of the last private pitched battle on English soil in the 15th Century when Lord Berkeley and Lord Lisle met in their long fight over the Berkeley inheritance.

Park near the Black Horse — the road opposite, The Street, is quite suitable — or if you plan to use the pub, then park in its car park, but please pop in and ask permission. If you want to go into the Tyndale monument when you reach it near the end of the walk, there is a key obtainable from the village shop, beyond the pub.
Adults 50p, Children 20p.
£2 deposit for the key.

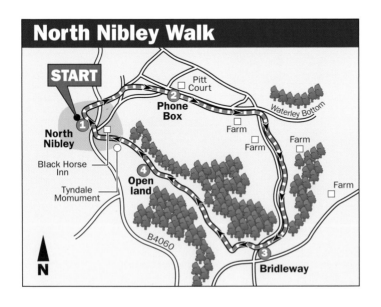

North Nibley Walk

① North Nibley - This is a pleasant, if not a typically picturesque Cotswold village, nestling below the escarpment and one of its claims to fame is the annual Lister-Petter Tyndale rally, held mid-June. This rally of Vintage Steam and Agricultural Vehicles, Classic Cars and Motorcyles, Military Vehicles, and Static engines, is staged on the nearby beautiful show ground.

Walk down The Street away from the village for a short distance to where there is a public footpath on each side of the road, just past a children's play area. Turn right on the path along a wire garden fence and the back of houses. Ahead are views of the wooded Cotswold edge. Follow the right fence, and then wall closely and drop down to a road. Cross straight over and go through a kissing gate opposite. Follow the footpath diagonally left in the field and about half way along the right edge go through a wooden gate and head along the edge of a woodland area. Go through another gate and continue on across a

small triangular field. Reach a lane and turn left, passing a nursery and gardens on your left.

Take the first footpath up on the right and go across the centre of the field parallel with the glorious wooded hill away on your left. Start to bear over to the left and leave the field in the far left corner, down a grassy track, through a gate to a lane in the small hamlet of Pitt Court by a phone box.

2 **Phone box** – Follow the lane towards Waterley Bottom. Stay on this for just over 0.75 miles to a crossroads. Turn right in the Wotton-under-Edge direction. (If you want a pub stop now, turn left on the lane and take the first right following signs to the New Inn – about ten minutes away uphill. It is a very popular Free House. Then return to this junction and go on the Wotton-under-Edge lane.)

After a few yards at a field entrance, look for the footpath which parallels the road on the left. It is up in the narrow band of woodland above the road. It eventually takes you left over a wooden stile barrier into a field. Turn right following the right

edge and leave in the corner through a 7-bar gate onto the lane again and continue on and up. (Or you can ignore the footpath and simply stay on the lane which gently winds its way uphill between grassy, ferny banks.)

Just as you near the top of the hill and the lane emerges from the woodland cover, turn right on a bridleway.

3 **Bridleway** – This goes along the right edge of a field pass a travellers' camp. Go through the metal barrier and turn left on a path along the edge of the woodland with field on your left. Make sure you follow these directions and don't stray off on other paths or you may get lost. Reach a T-junction with a broad crossing track. Turn right with woods on right and field on left. At a junction and clearing take the smaller path straight ahead through the woods. After about a third of a mile reach the end of the woods and a crossing track. Turn right and stay on the upper track – the Cotswold Way – soon going past a gate and through a grove of beautiful beeches.

4 **Open land** – Then come out onto open grassland high on the Cotswold edge with panoramic vistas. On the way up to the monument pass a topograph giving distances to various viewpoints. Reach the monument dedicated to William Tyndale.

He was a Gloucestershire lad, who first translated the Old and New Testaments of the Bible into English. He went to Oxford and became a great religious zealot, but who was eventually hunted down and martyred for his translation of the bible. Led out to the stake in Flanders in 1536, his last words were, "Lord, open the King of England's eyes", referring to Henry VII who had condemned Tyndale.

Take the path to the side of the monument, which drops down into the woodland. Go through a keyhole stile and Cotswold Way sign and go carefully down the steep path and steps. Turn left on the track at the bottom and follow it into North Nibley. Turn right to the Black Horse.

The Black Horse
North Nibley.
Call: 01453 546841

The New Inn
Waterley Bottom.
Call: 01453 543659

Watery ways

Cotswold Water Park: Near Cerney Wick –
Ashton Keynes – near Cerney Wick

About 7 miles. About 3.5 hours walking

OS Explorer Map, Cirencester and Swindon, ref: 063 962

Swans and other bird life are a feature of this flat and fascinating walk in the Cotswold Water Park, a man-made lakeland south of Cirencester in the area where the embryonic Thames flows. It is both a working and a

leisure landscape. There's quiet and peace in some areas with great bird watching. Elsewhere you can see sailors, canoeists, anglers, water skiers and also you encounter man at work still – as gravel extraction continues and old workings are turned into new lakes. Our circle is completely flat and easy on good paths, with some walking in fields near the end, but don't go after a lot of heavy rain as the first section in particularly may be flooded. There's a stop two-thirds of the way round at a good pub in the beautiful village of Ashton Keynes and then we head back on paths, across fields and alongside gravel working. It is an area that can change fairly quickly, but footpath diversions are well marked.

Cotswolds Water Park Walk

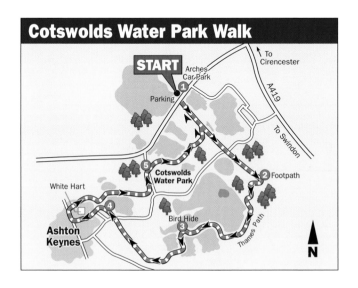

① Arches car park – Cross the main road carefully and take the path marked to Cricklade. Ignore any side paths and after about a mile go under more brick arches. On the left here is an attractive pond and garden with many specimen trees. Stay on the track for just over another half mile.

② Footpath – Then turn right on the clearly signed path to Ashton Keynes. It bends back on itself and then winds its way through pastureland and between lakes towards the village which is three miles distant. This is part of the long distance Thames Path.

③ Bird hide – After about two miles, pass a wooden bird hide on the right which is worth a visit with some interesting information about bird life in the area.

Not long after the bird hide you reach a t-junction with a track. Turn left following the Thames Path/Bridleway sign and shortly turn right on the marked Thames Path. If you reach a road you have gone too far.

Continue on across an area being land-scaped after gravel working – and gravel extraction still taking place not far away. Go through a kissing gate into Ashton Keynes Millennium Green and continue on following the path until it goes across the village sports field, and out the far side onto the road on the edge of Ashton Keynes.

④ **Ashton Keynes** - Once known as Essitone in the Domesday book, this village changed its names 10 times during the following 800 years. The people here lived off the fertile land – a community of

tradesmen serving the surrounding villages and the travellers on the road from Cirencester to Wootton Bassett which became a Turnpike in 1810. Many of the poorer people also took up glovemaking for the industry based in Circencester. With the newly spring Thames flowing through Ashton Keynes, it has always suffered from flooding. Today it is a beautiful village with many old houses and the Thames still flowing down the High Road.

Turn left a yard or two and then go right on the Thames Path between houses. Follow the path, ignoring side turns, until you come out through a kissing gate by Kent End Farm onto the end of a tarmac drive.

Here you have a choice – to continue our circle, or to take a short detour through the village to the welcoming White Hart.

Short route: Go across the entrance to the farm and follow the yellow arrow path marked to Cerney Wick.

For the pub: Go down to the road and turn left through the pretty village and take the first right into Fore Street and then go right in Park Place and at the end reach the White Hart which serves good snacks and meals and also has a garden.

(If you want to enjoy the village a little more and go to another pub, there's the renowned, award-winning old Horse and Jockey two minutes away down Gosditch opposite the White Hart.

Gosditch is the oldest street in the village. It is recorded that in the mid 19th Century one in the 35 homes in Gosditch Street lived a tailor, saddler, tallow chandler, stonemason, many glove makers

and a cobbler. The School was built in this street in 1870 and a Primitive Methodist chapel was opened in 1840, but became a baker's shop later. The Horse and Jockey was a "scrumpy house", selling cider made from apples from the orchards in the village an was the social centre of the community where dominoes were laid and gossip exchanged, and the hard times debated.

To continue: From the White Hart, turn right round the corner and follow the lane through the village. Turn right at the end on Back Lane. Go round the right corner into Kent End and then turn up left retracing your steps of earlier to the

tarmac drive at the entrance to Kent End Farm. Then go left on the footpath marked to Cerney Wick.

Follow the path which soon bends right by cottages and goes through a kissing gate. Turn right and come into an area which was being worked when I came here. Stay in this direction following footpath signs. Cross a gravel drive. You want to continue on in the same direction as before, but soon can pick up a fooptath on the right paralleling a gravel drive. It gets you away from the dusty lorries. At the end cross the gravel drive and follow the bridleway along the hedgeline with the busy road on your right. After about four minutes look for a stile on the right (broken when I was here) and come onto the main road.

⑤ Main road – Cross with care and turn left for about a minute. Then take the footpath to Cerney Wick over a stile on the right. It may be marked as a permissive path because of gravel working here. Go left with the road on your left and then follow it round right. Go left over a footbridge and then right going along the edge of a lake on the left. The path turns

left round the end of the lake and soon you see you are approaching another lake. Turn right (don't go up closely onto the grass by the lake). Continue on the path to the end and go left over a stile into a field. Go down the length of the field with woodland on your right and in the corner cross a stile onto a quiet lane.

Turn right for a few yards and go left on the Cerney Wick footpath over a stile. Follow the left edge of this field. Cross a stile and follow the right edge of the next field along and round. Reach a footbridge and cross to come onto the broad track you started out on. Turn left and retrace your steps back to the main road and the car park opposite.

White Hart
Ashton Keynes.
Call: 01285 861247

Horse and Jockey
Ashton Keynes.
Call: 01285 861270

Up hill & down dale

Pinbury Park – Edgeworth Manor – Daneway – Sapperton – Pinbury Park

6 miles, about 3 hours walking.

OS Explorer 168, Stroud, Tetbury & Malmesbury, ref: 962 057

Cotswold calm , contrasting combes and high open land, a serene tucked away church, a two mile long canal tunnel, plus a great country pub, are the ingredients of this unforgettable Gloucestershire circle between Stroud and Cirencester. There are also bluebells in the woods in season. It is very much a switchback walk – uphill and down dale as we progress in and out of valleys so there are steep sections.

START **near the Pinbury Park entrance.** Take the A419 Stroud to Cirencester road. If coming from Stroud, go through Chalford and after about 2.5 miles turn left towards Sapperton at Chapman's Cross by a big clump of trees on the corner. If coming from Cirencester, take the second turn right to Sapperton at Chapman's Cross. Go along here, over a crossroads and on for 2.8 miles from Chapman's Cross, ignoring side turns, to a signpost indicating the drive to Pinbury Park on the left. Continue on a little further to a black and white lodge house to Cirencester Park on the right and park anywhere now along this road on the verge... anywhere from here up to the crossroads about 0.75 mile away which is where we turn down when walking.

① **Pinbury Park entrance** – Walk along to the crossroads with the lane to Edgeworth, the lane to Duntisbourne Leer and Dangliworth. Turn left towards Edgeworth on the lane 'unsuitable for long vehicles'. Soon start to drop downhill into Golden Valley, formed by the River Frome. There are pleasant views over the valley and while still descending, take the marked bridleway on the left. This is a dry stony track dropping gently along the side of the hill.

Reach a gate and bridge over the Frome and come into the grounds of Edgeworth Manor. Turn right on the track uphill, going through a metal keyhole stile at the side of a gate. The beautiful grounds boast many daffodils and snowdrops in

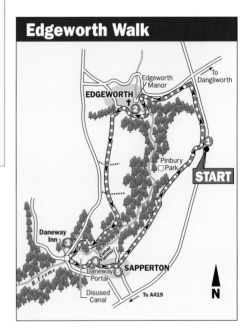

Edgeworth Walk

Spring, but are colourful throughout the year. Pass to the side of the manor house.

2 **Edgeworth Manor** - Continue on along the track and come out through a gate on to the entrance drive to the manor. Go left and shortly, opposite the church entrance, take the tarmac drive down on the left. But first visit the little church of St Mary. It has a medieval exterior and a restored Gothic Revival interior.

Notice the stone Cotswold stile to the left of the gate, which was probably there before the gate. See also the simple grave-stones lining the paths of the churchyard. There are more than 50 of them, almost all dating over a period of just 30 years from 1652 to 1682. At that time, only important people normally had stones, so it would seem that in this small village a local man must for 30 years have decided to provide cheap stones for everyone.

Of particular interest in the church is the 14th-Century stained-glass window in the chancel showing a bishop or archbishop, probably the martyred Thomas Becket. One of 13 miracles attributed to him and which led to his canonisation is said to have taken place at Edgeworth.

Take the tarmac drive which drops down opposite the church entrance. Go round the bend, passing a number of beautiful homes, to the end and through the gate marked with footpath arrows.

Go left on a grassy track for a few yards into the valley and then go ahead forking right uphill to a hunting gate up in the fence corner. Go through and follow the left boundary, continuing up to the top of the plateau and then ahead through fields, following the left wall. Keep on for about half a mile until you go through a hunting gate and reach a junction with a farm drive/track . Cross the track and follow the yellow footpath arrow across the field bearing left towards woodland.

Leave the field through a kissing gate and drop down into the woodland, bearing right.

At a broad crossing track in the woods, turn right and follow this for over half a mile, and then dropping down and coming out through a hunting gate on to a lane. Turn left to the Daneway Inn.

❸ **Daneway Inn** - Go through the car park of the inn and over a stile. Turn left following the well-used path with the river Frome on the right, although somewhat hidden at this point. Cross a stile into a nature reserve and continue along the path, noticing remains on the left of the disused Thames and Severn Canal.

Eventually reach a big arched entrance to a tunnel down on the canal bed on the left.

❹ **Daneway Portal** - This is the start of the two-mile long Sapperton Canal, which emerges at Coates. A path on the left takes you down for a good look

In 1788 King George III came to inspect the tunnel, built as part of the Thames-Severn canal link. Earlier this year the tunnel was visited by Prince Charles. This was the start of the Waterways Trust major fundraising appeal to restore the canal to some of its former glory.

Follow the path you were on and go up and over the canal tunnel and over a stile into a field. Go across the field, bearing up right to the top where you go through a kissing gate and take the path into the village.

As you reach the church, turn down left and go right into the churchyard. The church is certainly worth a visit.

It's an interesting building whose history and that of the village is explained in a guide book. The famous people who have links with Sapperton include Sir Stafford Cripps, Chancellor of the Exchequer after the World War Two who is buried in Sapperton Cemetery. John Masefield, the poet, lived for a time at nearby Pinbury Park which we are soon to pass. The church's pew ends come from panelling from the banqueting hall of Sapperton Manor House after it is was demolished in the 18th Century. There are two particularly noteworthy memorials —one to the Poole family in the north transept with Sir Henry Poole and his wife Anne surrounded by

their children, and the other in the south transept; a memorial to Sir Robert Atkyns, the historian who lived at Pinbury Park.

Leave the church up the main path under the ancient yews and through the gate on to the lane in Sapperton.

5 Sapperton - Sapperton means 'the home of the soap makers'. It is a reference to the former wool trade and the local extraction of fuller's earth, a special clay used for fulling (cleaning) the fleeces.

Cross and take the marked bridleway to the right of the telephone box.

Follow the path through a small field and go through a hunting gate and carry on along the side of the hill with the valley on your left. You are basically now going to stay in the same direction all the time, a distance of about 1.4 miles until you reach a drive to Pinbury Park.

As you go along on the right you will pass one of the entrances to the Bathurst Estate and the Bishop's Walk which is a horse ride. Continue on and drop down

a little and then on in the same direction as before under trees with a beautiful house down on the left. Enter another field with woodland on each side and then continue through the field, staying reasonably close to the band of woodland on the right.

At the end of the field, disregard the path which goes up right, and instead go ahead, bearing down left on a path and through a gate ahead into a field (ignoring the track left into the woods). Go across this field with Pinbury Park ahead, and curve to the right and then continue on gradually heading towards the drive. Drop down and pass a pond on the left and reach the drive. Turn right walking on the grass to the right side of the drive. Follow it all the way up to the end and go through a wooden gate in the corner onto the lane.

Turn left back to where you started.

The Daneway Inn
Call 01285 760297

The attractions of Ashleworth

Woolridge – Long Reach – Ashleworth – Longridge – Woolridge

About 4.5 miles (2.25 hours walking)

Ordnance Survey, Explorer 179 map, Gloucester, Cheltenham and Stroud, ref: 803 235

The unspoilt Boat Inn with sheltered courtyard tables on the river bank and freshly made filled baps will lure you to linger longer on this short circle north of Gloucester. We begin on a ridge, drop down and follow the edge of the Severn in elver fishing country to sleepy Ashleworth quay where there is not only the pub and pretty riverside location, but also an ancient tithe barn. Then we call in at Ashleworth village, with another pub option if you want more substantial refreshment.

There is a short drop down off the ridge near the start and then a steady climb back up on towards the end, but the rest is flat.

Walking is largely on grassy footpaths and tracks, some of the grass may be longish and wet and parts of the track a little uneven so you need good footwear.

START **on Woolridge.** From the A417 between Maisemore and Hartpury, take a very small turning called Hiams Lane on a bend by a bus shelter. From Gloucester if you reach the turning left to Hartpury College you have gone too far, and conversely if coming from Hartpury, pass the College turn and look for Hiams Lane on the bend on the left. Follow this narrow lane up and past the Rising Sun on the right and then find somewhere suitable to park on the side where you won't obstruct gates or other cars. There is a reasonable choice – especially if you go to the junction and turn left on the Over Old Road in the direction of Hartpury and Ledbury for a short distance to find somewhere along the roadside. We walk along this road so it doesn't matter where you park – it will either shorten the beginning or end of your walk. Don't park in the Rising Sun car park. The friendly landlady explained that she often shuts the gates after closing hours so her horses can graze the grass around the pub and she doesn't want anyone leaving the gates open.

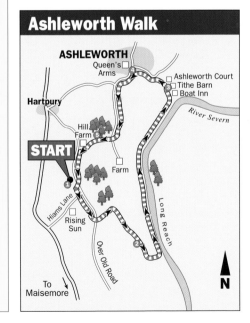

Ashleworth Walk

1 **Woolridge** – Begin the walk along Over Old Road. If you are parked near the Rising Sun go up to the junction and turn right. If parked along the Over Old Road itself then turn south in the Gloucester direction. There are good views from the ridge over the Vale of Gloucester. Drop downhill and take the first marked footpath on the left. Go along with the hedge on your left and then follow the track round right at the end. Follow the fence along the edge of the hill, passing a pond down below and continuing on.

Go through two tall kissing gates and then ahead along the grassy ridge with views towards Gloucester.

2 **End of hill** – Drop fairly steeply off the end of the ridge and go down to a wooden kissing gate by a larger gate. Turn left on the track and then almost immediately go right on the footpath down the side of a field.

At the end with the river ahead of you (it may be obscured by a hedge) turn left, – again following the right of way arrow.

Follow the river through several fields on the track for about 1.3 miles. Go over three stiles and reach the Riverboat Inn on the edge of Ashleworth.

Staying unmodernised and maintaining good service and friendliness have won this small pub many awards. Fresh, tasty baps are served in a separate building near the river by Jackie Jelf whose family has unbelievably run the pub since the 16th Century! She and husband Ron are carrying on the tradition. The family also used to run the ferry service across the Severn here. The choice for sitting is the cosy pub interior, the courtyards, benches by the river or sit yourself down on the riverbank itself. If you want a quiet drink, try and avoid the annual Beer Festival at the pub in September! Ring for dates.

From the pub walk up the road and soon pass Ashleworth Old Barn.

❸ Tithe Barn – This remarkable and rare barn in the care of the National Trust dates back to 1492-7 by Abbot Newland from St Augustine's Abbey in Bristol. Originally it had two identical barn spaces separated by a partition which was rare and the reason is a little uncertain – perhaps it was to store two different crops at the same time.

At the side of the barn go down the path and visit the church which sits alongside beautiful 15th Century Ashleworth Court, which is still a working farm.

This stone manor house together with the church and the barn form a unique group of medieval buildings near the Severn.

Continue up the road to a T-junction and turn left to the green in Ashleworth village.

4 **Ashleworth** - Here we go left, but if you want a fuller lunch then turn right for a few yards to the Queens Arms, another very attractive pub.

To continue, go out of the village on the Hartpury, Gloucester Road. After about five minutes, go left on the No Through Road, Longridge Lane. As you go along here you pass two or three beautiful cottage restorations that are in progress. Opposite the third one, Field Barn, go right through a wooden field gate on the marked bridleway.

Head up the field quite steeply stopping to enjoy the views as you ascend and in the top near the left hand corner go through a wooden hunting gate into woodland.

5 **Wood** - It may be muddy around the gate due to cattle. Follow the path up the left side of the wood, again quite steeply, and near the top go through a gate and ahead along a wide grassy track towards a farm. Go through a gate and pass the farmhouse on your right and go through another gate onto the lane, Over Old Road. Turn left along the ridge enjoying views across the Severn Vale and to the Cotswolds and in the other direction towards the Forest of Dean and find you way back to where you began.

The Boat Inn
Call: 01452 700272
Serves baps only.

The Queen's Arms
Ashleworth.
Call: 01452 700272
Open for lunches – during the winter, Tuesday, Fridays and weekends; from Easter every day except Monday.

Cromwell's Lookout

Hailes Abbey – Ford – Hailes Abbey

7.5 miles, 3.5 hours walking

Map: OS Outdoor Leisure 45, The Cotswolds Reference: 050 300

This is a real North Cotswold charmer, starting at a ruined abbey and exploring the rolling hills and valleys with a stop at a renowned pub half-way round. There are stunning views, particularly from an Iron Age hill fort above Hailes Abbey. Walking is on quiet lanes and the Cotswold and Gloucestershire Ways. It is not particularly strenuous although naturally there are hills to climb. Reward yourself with tea at the end.

START **Hailes Abbey is off the B4632 road between Winchcombe and Broadway.** Park in the Abbey visitors car park by the small church or in the overspill park. I left the pleasures of the abbey until the end but you may decide to do otherwise.

① **Hailes Abbey** – Founded in 1246 and once a celebrated pilgrimage site, this Cistercian abbey lies in ruins following its demolition in the 16th Century under the reign of Henry VIII. It was popular with medieval pilgrims because it reputedly housed a vial of Christ's blood. Remains of the dramatic cloister arches survive and there is a small museum worth visiting.

From the small car park by the church, cross the drive on to the Cotswold Way towards Winchcombe. Pass the abbey remains on your left and head for the far-right corner. Pass through a gate and down a drive to a lane. Turn left and follow this gently climbing lane, with great views across the valley, for about three-quarters of a mile. It is a steady uphill stretch of about 12 minutes. Turn left on the drive/public footpath to Little Farmcote Farm.

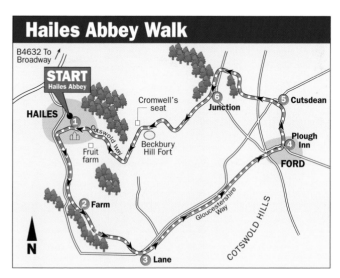

Hailes Abbey Walk

❷ Farm – Cross the farm cattle grid and walk through the farmyard. You are now on the Gloucestershire Way. Turn left into a field before a big barn then right along the top of the field. Keep on when the fence ends and head up to the far-top corner. Continue in the next field along the side of the hill. Eventually the track brings you into an area of bushes and small trees. Pass through and out into a field. Follow the arrow over a metal barrier and follow the right hedge. Cross a stile, pass a barn and continue along the track along the edge of the hill. A gate brings you to a lane. Turn left.

❸ Lane – Stay on Ford Lane for over mile, climbing gently then undulating and finally dropping downhill into horsey country. Pass Slade Barn and take the marked Gloucestershire Way on the right, which is fenced for quite a way, goes down, then climbs steadily out of the valley Stay on the path, first between hedges, then with a quarry on the left and field on the other side. Come into another field and follow the hedge on the right. There are good views from this high vantage point across to Farmcote. Then, as you

drop down, begin to see Ford below. At the bottom, walk out onto a lane. Turn left and immediately right on a short permissive path parallel with the road. Drop down onto the main road and turn right into Ford hamlet – about 1.5 hours into the walk.

❹ Plough Inn – Reach the 16th Century Plough Inn.

Note the welcoming verse to weary travellers on the wall outside! The pub is open all day, serving coffee, lunches and cream teas later. It is a beautiful and well-maintained old inn with a good garden.

Cross the road and take the marked Gloucestershire Way opposite. Walk along

the Tarmac drive for a short distance between horse gallops and paddocks, then left on the marked path between paddocks. At the end, turn right under a line of rowan trees. Cross a stile into a pretty meadow and follow the arrows down the length of the field then across to the far-left corner and over a stile.

Turn left up the edge towards the church and Cutsdean hamlet. Go through an opening by a metal gate and a short way along the left wall then left into the churchyard. It is a pretty church with a wonderful east window. Continue out the other side into a farmyard and right to the lane on the edge of the hamlet.

⑤ Cutsdean – Turn left away from the hamlet. Ignore a turn right and shortly, just by the Cutsdean sign, turn right on the marked footpath through woodland. Climb a stile/ barrier and walk along by the right hedge. Cross a similar barrier and cross straight over a lane. Climb a stile, followed by another and walk uphill by the left hedge. At the top, turn right with woodland, Carey's Covet, on your left. Walk all the way to the corner then left through a gate. A short track leads into a field. Follow the left hedge straight on.

In the corner, climb a metal barrier and a stone stile. Cross a lane and take the stile opposite. Now follow the footpath, which parallels the lane through woodland, a field and more woodland until you come out onto the lane and turn right. There were nettles near the end of the path when I came here, so if you are wearing shorts stay on the lane.

⑥ Junction – Reach a junction with the main road. Cross and take the left-hand Cotswold way path marked to Hailes Abbey. Follow the broad dry track for about a third of a mile. On the way pass a small walled compound on the right with a distinctive black barn raised up on staddle stones.

At the entrance to a small wooded quarry, turn right on the Cotswold Way. Come into a field and follow the arrow along the right wall. Follow it round the corner and enjoy glorious views across the Vale of Evesham from this Cotswold edge.

through a gate and cross this next field, bearing slightly right and following the Cotswold Way arrows until you cross a stile on to a broad crossing track.

Turn right and follow it down to Hailes Fruit Farm, which is a short walk down a drive on the left.

Continue to the second corner and through a gate. Follow the right edge on, as before, and reach a raised long mound and earthworks on the left. This dramatic spot is the site of the Iron Age hill fort of Beckbury Camp.

There is a farm shop selling local products, including apple juice and cider, and a cafe.

Return to the track you were on and continue on down (now on tarmac) back to Hailes Abbey where the National Trust has a shop and tea room.

Carry on and leave the field at the end to come to a stone monument, stunningly sited on the edge of the escarpment.

It is known as Cromwell's Seat but its history is shrouded in mystery. It is thought to date from the 18th Century and it is said that Cromwell sat here and watched Hailes Abbey being destroyed but of course the date isn't right for that.

Plough Inn

Ford.

Call: 01386 584215

Hailes Abbey

Is open from 10am – 6pm

from April to end of September

(open to 5pm until the end of October)

Go steeply down a path under beeches then bear left on the Cotswold Way across a field, dropping gently. Pass

Simply breathtaking

**May Hill village hall – Glasshouse – Clifford's Mesne –
May Hill – May Hill village hall**

About 6.9 miles. about 3.25 hours walking.

OS Outdoor Leisure Map 14, Wye Valley & Forest of Dean, ref: 708 208

On a good clear day, there is nothing to beat the 360 degree view from the National Trust's grassy May Hill in Gloucestershire. It is simply breathtaking and well worth quite a steep climb. When I came it was also a haze of blue from the bluebells not only

in the woodland but also right on top where the area has been cleared. It would be an ideal picnic spot, and afterwards there is a gentle downhill stretch back to the start. From the hamlet of Glasshouse, we go through the attractive mixed woodland of Newent Woods, good under foot, except for perhaps a couple of boggy sections. We follow footpaths and quiet lanes and pass the National Birds of Prey Centre and then a gentle climb on tracks to Clifford Mesne, a hamlet of scattered cottages. Then a drink outside on the terrace of the Yew Tree Inn would be pleasant before the uphill stretch to May Hill, the pièce de résistance of this memorable circle. It is an ideal dog circle too.

START at **May Hill Village Hall which on the map is just south of the hamlet of Glasshouse.** From Gloucester take the A40 towards Ross on Wye and after about 9.5 miles, go through Huntley and after another mile, look for the right fork to Glasshouse. Follow this lane for 0.75 miles to the village hall and car park on the right. If it is full, find somewhere near to park.

1 **May Hill Hall** – Turn right from the car park and along the lane, soon getting good views across to the Malverns and the Cotswolds with the Severn Valley in between. Very shortly reach a junction – with the war memorial cross on your left. Turn right and after a few minutes come down to the junction at Glasshouse with the tempting inn, noted for its draught beers. Note the remarkable topiary hedge on the left shaped like a cottage.

Turn left on the Clifford Mesne road for three minutes and take the marked public footpath right over a stile. Go across the field, bearing slightly right, and over a stile into Newent Woods which you will walk through for about the next mile. Go ahead

a few yards to a clearing after forestry work and then take the second track on the right. The wood was full of bird song and bird activity when I walked here. After about four minutes, turn left on a crossing track marked as path 170. It is a bridleway and you may have to negotiate some boggy, muddy sections although there are ways around the side. Stay on the 170 straight over another crossing track.

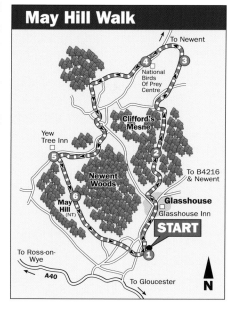

May Hill Walk

❷ **Pond** - Reach a pond, Huntley Pools, and pass it on your left and climb gently uphill to a cleared area of the woods. We want to go more or less straight ahead but the way to do it is to go right on the track for a short distance and then bear left on another track, so you are back on course. There we see bluebells and stitchwort along here and promises of foxgloves to come. After about 250 yards, look over to the right and see a large shed with corrugated roof behind trees. Stay on the track through older woodland.

At a bungalow and sheds, turn left on the track/drive and come to a lane.

Turn right and soon go under a double row of very prominent power lines which stride out uncompromisingly across this part of the country. Go to the side of a cattle grid and entrance to Green Farm passing the beautiful farmhouse on your right. Opposite a farm barn, go left through the marked gate and down fairly close to the right hedge. A resident swan was ruling the roost down on the pond on the left and causing a lot of commotion!

Go over a stile by a gate and follow the path with a stream and garlic woods on the left. Cross a stile and drop down into a new orchard.

❸ Orchard – Go ahead down between a line of fruit trees and at the end reach the edge of the stream again. After a few yards cross left over the new footbridge. Follow the arrow right for about 30 yards and go through a kissing gate. Immediately go left up the fence of the field with paddock on your left towards a red brick house passing it on your left. Another metal kissing gate brings you to the lane.

Turn left and after four minutes reach the renowned National Birds of Prey Centre.

❹ Birds of Prey Centre – This is home to one of the most significant birds of prey collection in the world with about 85 species. There are flying demonstrations at different times. No dogs are allowed

and you can only go into the café or shop if you have paid for entry.

Carry on along the lane for a few more minutes and pass the Clifford Mesne village sign. Ignore a footpath and after a few more yards turn right up the track by the house. Continue on this going uphill, and ignore a track going left. The track runs into a tarmac drive by a house. Continue on, more or less on the flat now. After a few minutes reach a bend and go straight ahead on the grassy track, ignoring a stile on the right. At a junction of tracks, near a cottage, take the bridleway which is second left. This is a pleasant old track going along the edge of the hill with good views over to the right at gate openings and gaps.

Reach a tarmac lane/drive and continue on. Join a lane where you turn right and after a few yards reach a junction. Go right and then left on the Glasshouse lane. Follow it down to a junction at the bottom and turn right, still towards Glasshouse.

5 **Yew Tree Inn** – Turn right again up to the Yew Tree which has a gloriously sited terrace at the side and serves very tasty food. There is quite a climb ahead so bear this in mind when ordering food!

Continue past the Yew Tree starting the first part of the steady climb up to May Hill.

May Hill and May Hill Common owned by the National Trust is an Area of Outstanding Natural Beauty and a Site of Special Scientific Interest. It is an area of grassy, heather and wild flowers and home to the tree pipit and yellow hammer. Look out for the small copper butterfly in summer.

Enter the National Trust area through a gate by the cattle grid, ignore the footpath left, and stay on the lane which levels out soon and gives you pleasant views. After about half a mile from where you left the pub, reach a marked public footpath on either side of the lane. Go left and continue straight on up through bracken, birches and bluebells. Turn left on a crossing grassy track which takes you on up. Go through a kissing gate and continue up on the more open grassy land to the top passing to the left of a clump of pines at the top of May Hill.

6 Top of May Hill – Behind the pines them is a trig point at 296 metres and from here the views are superb.

Continue in the same direction ahead past the pines on what is now the 100 miles long Gloucestershire Way which we follow almost all the way back to where we started.

We start to descend and go down through a gate marking the end of the National Trust area. Continue on downhill. At a junction keep straight over on the Gloucestershire Way. When the track forks, take the one ahead (not left). Stay on the main track, ignore a turn right and come down to a lane by a cottage. Turn right a few yards and then left on the Gloucestershire Way still dropping downhill. Come alongside a cottage and onto a tarmac drive and carry on down to a lane. Take the Gloucestershire Way opposite over a stile and down the beautiful field with lovely views. Cross a stile by a gate at the bottom and come onto a drive by another cottage. Turn left down here, passing a pond, and reach the lane. Here we leave the Gloucestershire Way and turn left on the lane, reaching May Hill Village Hall after about five minutes.

The Glasshouse Inn
Call: 01452 830454

The Yew Tree Inn
Is an attractive pub restaurant which serves home cooked, high quality light and full meals (no crisps or sandwiches). Closed all day Monday and Sunday evenings, and only full meals at Sunday lunch.
Call: 01531 820719

National Birds of Prey Centre
open February to November.
Call: 0870 990 1992
website: www.npbc.co.uk.

'Pilgrimage' to the healing well

Nine Wells car park − Parkhouse − Trellech − Nine Wells

5.75 miles. 3 hours walking

OS Outdoor Leisure 14, Wye Valley, ref: 513 038

Wandering through the Wye valley on this relaxing and quiet walk − off the main beat of walkers − will uplift the spirits. It is easy going mainly on dry tracks and quiet lanes with no steep hills. Apart from a great pub at Trellech, there are some ancient standing stones to visit and a healing well that attracted pilgrims for centuries. . The Wye Valley is one of Britain's most important Areas of Outstanding Natural Beauty straddling the English − Welsh border. As you will see on this circle, it is a living and working landscape.

START at Nine Wells car park. Go to Tintern and turn at the side of the Wye Valley Hotel on the road to Catbrook. Ignore the turn to Catbrook and continue on to a junction. Turn left towards Trellech. Stay on this for nearly a mile, ignoring a left turn. Just before a junction look for the car park tucked in on the left.

❶ Nine Wells car park – Go out the back through the yellow and green barrier and follow the dry forest track, ignoring side turns, for nearly a mile. Go over two step stiles and the path ends by taking you over a stone slab stile onto a lane. Turn left.

Shortly take the first footpath on the right (opposite a track on left). Go to the end and over a slab stile into a field. Follow the left fence ahead and then left round the corner. Then cross another stone stile into woodland. The path goes ahead and at

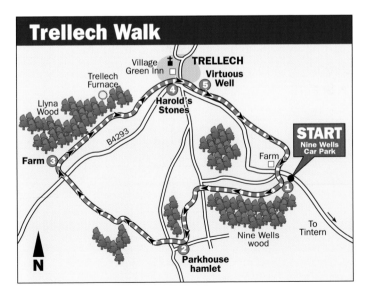

Trellech Walk

Village Green Inn
Trellech Furnace
Llyna Wood
TRELLECH
Virtuous Well ❺
Harold's Stones
❹
B4293
Farm ❸
START
Nine Wells Car Park
Farm
❶
Nine Wells wood
To Tintern
❷
Parkhouse hamlet
N

the end bends left to a stile. Follow the fenced path to a road, with views through the trees over the valley.

2 **Parkhouse hamlet** – You are now in the tiny hamlet of Parkhouse. Turn right downhill. Go straight over a T-junction and continue downhill on the No Through road. Continue on, passing a Welsh Water Treatment Works. Cross a stream on stepping stones and turn left alongside the stream. Follow the track as it bends right and climbs up out of the valley quite gently.

Come to a farm. Go through the gate, through the farm and out the other side on the tarmac drive. Reach the main road. Cross and take the drive/track opposite to another farm.

3 **Farm** – At the farm, turn right on the marked path to Trellech (2.2kms), through the second gate on the right. Go through two fields along the right fence and at the end of the second field drop down to a gate by trees. Go straight ahead in the next field parallel with the woods. On the other side, follow a yellow

footpath arrow by a large oak on a fence corner which directs you down into the woods. Go through a hunting gate and down over a wooden bridge and then up into the field and straight on along the left fence. Reach a waymark post.

There is an optional path on the left down through woods to the ruins of Trellech Furnace which used to produce pig iron in the late 17th Century. It's nearly a mile and the path is overgrown.

To continue our walk, go in the Trellech direction, over a stile, and ahead in the field with woods over left. Drop down to another waymark sign and go left to Penarth Brook. Cross and immediately go right on the small path along the brook. You can stay close to the stream or shortly go up a little away and pick up a track. In any event, follow the stream on

your right. Cross a stile by a gate and take the track to the main road. Turn left and shortly come to the standing stones on the right.

❹ **Harold's Stones** – The village of Trellech gets its name from these three stones. 'Tre or tri' meaning three and 'lech' meaning stone. The stones, set in a 12m line, date back 3,500 years to the Bronze Age and are of conglomerate rock called 'Pudding Stone'. They were dragged to the site on logs and levered into position either for seasonal information or for use at religious ceremonies.

Carry on along the road. Our walk continues by going right on the road to Llandogo, Catbrook and Tintern, but it is well worth a couple of minutes detour into Trellech.

On the left pass a sign directing you to Tump Turret which dates back to Norman times and may have been the site of a castle, erected during the reign of Henry I.

In the Middle Ages Trellech was an important settlement with a population comparable with those of Cardiff and Newport. There were over 300 land holdings or burgages. The destruction of over 100 of the landholdings during the Welsh rebellion in 1295 started the decline of Trellech and in 1314 the Earl of Gloucester whose land included Trellech, was killed at the Battle of Bannockburn and his landholding split up. Then in the 14th Century the Black Death killed off a third of the population.

Reach the Village Green, a very welcoming inn and restaurant where prices are very reasonable.

If you visit the church, note the preaching cross outside dating from the 8th or 9th Century. The church is an example of early Gothic work and its' large size reflects the former size of Trellech. Of interest inside is the sundial near the font at the west end, and originally outside. Three local places of interest are recorded on the plinth, the

Tump, Harold's Stones and Virtuous Well (you will soon visit).

Retrace your steps and take the Llandogo road, immediately taking the first left turn. A few minutes along this road reach Virtuous Well on the left.

⑤ Virtuous Well - Once called St Ann's Well, this has attracted pilgrims right up to the 17th Century because of its healing powers. There are four separate springs, three of which are rich in iron, and each said to cure a different disease.

Stay on the road for about ten minutes. Pass a left turn and shortly go left up Woodway Drive which is a right of way. Follow it past the bungalow and continue along the stony path through woods. Reach the ornamental gate to Cleddon Hall and turn right on the track. Cross the road taking the tarmac lane opposite to reach the main road and the Nine Wells car park opposite.

The Village Green Inn and Restaurant
Trellech.
Call: 01600 869180